THINGS WE WISH OUR *Parents* KNEW

ANONYMOUS LETTERS FROM TEENAGERS
THAT INSPIRE COURAGEOUS CONVERSATIONS

THINGS WE WISH OUR *Parents* KNEW

MICHAEL CHIASSON

GREENLEAF
BOOK GROUP PRESS

Published by Greenleaf Book Group Press
Austin, Texas
www.gbgpress.com

Distributed by Greenleaf Book Group

For ordering information or special discounts for bulk purchases, please contact Greenleaf Book Group at PO Box 91869, Austin, TX 78709, 512.891.6100.

Design and composition by Greenleaf Book Group
Cover design by Greenleaf Book Group
Cover images used under license from ©Adobestock.com

Publisher's Cataloging-in-Publication data is available.

Print ISBN: 979-8-88645-387-4

eBook ISBN: 979-8-88645-388-1

To offset the number of trees consumed in the printing of our books, Greenleaf donates a portion of the proceeds from each printing to the Arbor Day Foundation. Greenleaf Book Group has replaced over 50,000 trees since 2007.

Printed in Canada on acid-free paper

25 26 27 28 29 30 31 32 10 9 8 7 6 5 4 3 2 1

First Edition

You are braver than you believe, stronger than you seem, smarter than you think, and loved more than you will ever know.

—Winnie the Pooh

Contents

ACKNOWLEDGMENTS

When gratitude becomes the anthem of our generation, generosity will be seen in everything that we do. I believe this to the very core of who I am. I have seen it displayed time and time again as students begin to see the beautiful truth about themselves. It has been more than twenty-five years since I began my career as a communicator, and never in a million dreams would I have imagined how incredible this journey would become. The start to this project is only the beginning of helping give this generation of students a way to be seen, heard, and encouraged.

I start these acknowledgments by honoring every student who took time to share their heart with all of us. I thank them for trusting me and for allowing me to share my heart with them. Each and every one of them has made a contribution they can be proud of. Though their stories may still have many challenges that need to be faced, their willingness and courage to share what they have shared is a remarkable act of generosity. I hope they remember that their track record for getting through bad days is 100 percent, and I believe that the best is yet to come for them. I am their champion and will continue to help their voices be heard.

As I reflect on how to honor the countless number of people who have believed in me over the years, I am terrified of leaving someone out. So, to be as clear and to the point as I can be, my life is overflowing with gratitude and love for every one of my friends, family members, supporters, colleagues, teachers, coaches, and mentors.

There are, of course, a great many people who have helped make this project move from an idea to a reality.

First, I thank you for reading this book. Whether you are a student, parent, grandparent, teacher, or guide, my hope for you is that you never forget the important role you have as a hero for this next generation. Because of you, the world is better and a whole lot brighter.

With a grateful heart, I thank my team, both past and present: Alix, Tanya, Maria, Caroline, Natalie, Johnny, Andrew, Demetrio, Corey, Mark, Haley, Daniel, Christine, Jimmy, Chris, Steve, Audrey, Peter, John, Ryan, Dawson, Rikka, Eric, Beverley, Vince, Stephen, Adrian, Jason, Dave, Joe, Trevor, Henry, Theresa, Lorne, Joel, Yuan, Kaya, Elliot, Matthew, and Melissa.

I will forever be grateful for my journey with all the school districts across Canada and beyond that have welcomed my team and me to serve their school communities. I am every teacher's, support staffer's, custodian's, administrator's, trustee's, and director's biggest supporter. I am honored that together we are *inspiring the world one student at a time.*

I thank my tribe—Matthew, Aaron, Bishop Sam, Fr. J, Fr. Troy, the Warrens, the Klassens, the Cichons, the Jarrells, the Catlings, the Wolf Pack, and the Eberley crew—for their honesty, friendship, encouragement, and guidance.

I thank Kathy Jarrell, Kimberly Cichon, Season Eberley, Doug McNeil, Dr. Kevin McNeil, Dr. Hossein, Hilary Vos, Aaron and

Victoria Hoddinott, and Sharon Van der Sloot. Their patience and direction have made this all possible.

Many years ago, this process started with the talented Cheryl Stebbins. Her care and guidance taught me the art of patience when it comes to writing a book. I thank her for her help and encouragement to start the process. Ryan Factura's ability to take the vision I have and make it real is a gift I am in awe of. His support and example inspire me to always work to make it better. I thank him for always being available and, most importantly, for his friendship. Aryn Kalson-Sperandio's patience and love for me and this project have inspired and helped me to complete this book, which was years in the making. She has been a joy to work with. I thank her for the countless hours of care and attention to detail that she sacrificed to make this possible.

I thank Greenleaf Book Group for seeing the value of this project. Their team has been incredible to work with. From my first welcome call to the support team with Rebecca and Leah, I am honored to have had them with me in this process.

As I sit here in my office, I am overwhelmed with gratitude for my partners. It is because of them that my team and I are able to do what we do best. With every sacrifice they have made to support me and our mission, we have been able to bring a message of hope and encouragement to hundreds of thousands of students and parents across North America. I thank them for their continued generosity and support.

I thank my parents for the gift of my life. Looking back, I now see the sacrifices they both made to support me the best they could. I miss my dad and the joy he brought everywhere he went. I am grateful to my mom for her example of never giving up and for showing me that there is always a way.

I believe heaven kissed earth the day my kids, Hannah and Simon, were born. Melissa and I are so proud of them and will forever be their greatest champions. I love them both with all my heart and will continue to spend my life showing them how much they both mean to me. And though our son Jacob was with us for only a short time, we will forever remember and cherish the twenty-four minutes we had together.

I saved the best for last. In the summer of 2005, my wife, Melissa, promised her love to me, and I am still wrapping my head around the thought that I could be the recipient of a gift so beautiful, so generous, so faithful and wise. She has taught me how to be loved and to love deeper. I am thankful to wake up next to her and know that whatever comes our way, our faith, hope, and love for each other will be the anchor that makes our days to come better and brighter than we could ever imagine.

Here's to a future that our kids will be grateful for.

INTRODUCTION

We are shaped by stories that have come before us. Of that, we are certain. Also, we are shaped by stories as we live through them. However, I believe the greatest impact we can make in our lifetime is being intentional in the way we accompany those whose well-being is entrusted to our care as their greatest influence—our children—because that will shape the stories they live and get to tell in the future. It is my sincere hope that this book will help you in that.

In the following pages of *Things We Wish Our Parents Knew*, I invite you to walk with me as I share with you a bit about my life—just as those thousands of students have shared with me a bit of theirs.

Born and raised in Houston, Texas, in many ways I experienced a typical upbringing. But my journey has also taken me through the depths of childhood trauma, the complexities of mental illness, the honest (and often painful) pursuit of understanding, and the reality of hope and healing.

From an early age, I faced a familiar path that many can relate to. When I was three, my parents divorced. I was shattered. Primarily under the care of my father, I found myself navigating the uncharted territories of life without the foundation of stability I had known.

My mother, a remarkable woman who battled mental illness throughout her life, faced her own arduous journey. The lack of her needs being met and the unspeakable abuse she experienced as a child led her to search for love and acceptance wherever she could find it. My dad was a musician and life of the party. He was carefree, generous, and always made you feel that you were the most important person in the room. I can see why my mother was drawn to him. Once they got together, it wasn't long after that my mom was pregnant, and I was on the way. Though this came as a surprise, they decided (without much thought) that they should get married.

For my mother, the idea of being married was everything she had dreamed of, but what was required for the relationship to work was an investment both of them were unwilling to make. My mom's trauma from previous relationships and my dad's hip lifestyle and history of infidelity was a ticking time bomb. Two independent people with very strong personalities were confronted with an invitation to love each other in good times and bad, sickness and health, but ultimately their spoken vows were only words that sounded great at the altar of their decision.

To this day, my relationship with my mother is still not where I hope it could be. I lived with her until the end of second grade. During this time, I was exposed to things that as an adult I am still working through to understand. This included emotional, mental, and sexual abuse that I've lived through—committed by individuals my mother entrusted to my care. It was the people she lived with, as well as friends and babysitters, who took from me my innocence and distorted my view of women and men for many years to come.

As a kid, I did not know how to process these experiences, but the most difficult part was watching my mother struggle in finding her place and purpose. Unfortunately, the path she chose landed her in prison multiple times. I have heard it said that kids do not stop loving their parents because of their mistakes and failures—instead, they stop loving themselves.

I am, however, thankful for the many gifts that my mother shared with me. Though the decisions she made created a difficult path for me to walk, my mom is a fighter. She has always been able to find a way to make it through her darkest days, and I have found this to be one of the great gifts she taught me.

The echoes of the trauma I experienced in those early years continue to reverberate through my life today. However, I refuse to be defined solely by the struggles I have faced. It is within the depths of these experiences that I have discovered a profound purpose—to share my journey of healing and growth, to hopefully illuminate the path for others, and most importantly, to help deepen the connections between parents and their children.

Many years later, after completing high school, I moved to Alberta, Canada, to attend college. This was the beginning of a new chapter that would eventually lead me to be with you today. After finishing college, I was honored to be asked to play guitar for an artist whose career was about to take off. Now, as an aside, I've played music professionally since the age of fourteen, and this was one of the great gifts that my dad passed on to me. He was an accomplished musician himself; however, he didn't like to talk about that too much. He played in circles with Jerry Lee Lewis, Roy Orbison, Johnny Winter, and to my shock and awe, Elvis Presley. Though his music career was not long, music was always a big part of our lives growing up. As a single father, I see now the heroic sacrifices he made for me, to create the best life possible that he could provide.

That life, of course, was far from perfect—but looking back on it, I don't think any of us require perfection as much as we long for connection, and connection was one of my dad's superpowers.

As I continued to tour as a musician throughout Canada, we had a concert in a city in Alberta called Calgary. It was November 2003, and that was when I met the greatest and most beautiful person I had ever seen. This person revealed to me a definition of love I had never known. Melissa and I were married in 2005, and today we still live in the prairies of Alberta and have the privilege of being the parents of two beautiful children who are with us today. But this has not come without a struggle. As you will read in a later chapter, at the beginning of our marriage, my wife was diagnosed with a sickness that was completely unexpected, followed by the loss of our first son, Jacob. The encore to this painful chapter in our life was the sickness I was diagnosed with, which was the beginning of the road that led me to be with you here today. (I want to mention that today, both Melissa and I are completely healthy and clear, and our children, Hannah and Simon, are doing great as we are learning, like you, how to navigate the roller coaster of parenting.)

It was during this time that the seeds of our charity were planted—a heartfelt initiative aimed at helping students better understand themselves and parents better understand the inner worlds of their children.

Those seeds finally came into fruition in 2009 when we founded a Canadian-registered charity that has become a beacon of hope and understanding for families across the country. Each year, we have the privilege of engaging with thousands of students, parents, and teachers. Through immersive event experiences, conferences, seminars, and interactive programs, we strive to empower both students and parents, providing them with the tools and insights necessary to navigate the often-turbulent times of adolescence.

The approach I have taken in this book mirrors the way I speak to students—authentic, relatable, and grounded in my personal experiences. Throughout these pages, you will find a collection of anecdotes and reflections drawn from the stories and lessons I have encountered along my own journey. Through the sharing of these experiences, I hope to instill a sense of connection and familiarity for you, with the intent to remind you of the miracle of your own story and the gift you are to the kids you are guiding.

One of the most powerful elements of the work I do stems directly from the students we serve—the very people whose voices are often unheard. As an integral part of our mission, we invited students to anonymously share their story through heartfelt letters prompted by "Things I wish my parents knew." To date, we have received more than five thousand letters—a testament to our profound impact and the clear need that every parent, grandparent, coach, guide, and mentor could benefit from.

Throughout this book, you will have the privilege of reading portions of these powerful letters, providing a glimpse into the raw emotions, desires, needs, and struggles that young people are facing today. Their words will serve as a reminder that the yearning for understanding and connection transcends age and circumstance. It is important to note that the letters we have received have not come from any one-on-one sessions. Our student events are geared toward grades six through twelve, with a range of one hundred to twelve hundred students in attendance at a time, and the students have the option, if they choose, to write an anonymous letter during the event or shortly after its conclusion.

At the end of each chapter, you will encounter sections titled "Accept," "Reflect," and "Connect." This framework represents the core philosophy of our work, guiding both parents and children toward accepting the reality of what they are facing, reflection on their experiences within that reality, and ultimately, creating a deeper connection with one another. Through this shared journey of accepting, reflecting, and connecting, my desire is to encourage both sides to start the courageous conversations that will ensure our kids are seen, heard, understood, and loved.

In closing, I want to extend my gratitude to you, the parents who will journey alongside me within these pages. Your willingness to explore the complexities of parenting, to grasp a better understanding of your children's experiences, and to bridge the gap of communication and connect with them is remarkable. You are the heroes, the awakeners, and the catalyst of change for good. Your commitment to growth and connection is a gift that will echo throughout your children's future.

Above all, I invite you to remember that the path to understanding and connection is not without its challenges. It requires patience, humility, grace, and a genuine desire to truly see and hear your children. Embrace this vulnerability and open your hearts to the unspoken truths that lie within them. Through the power of honesty, courage, reflection, and connection, you will make a difference that will withstand the tests of time.

In the end, it is my sincere hope that the stories, reflections, and insights shared within this book will ignite a spark within you—a spark that illuminates the miracle that has been entrusted to you and fuels deeper conversations between you and your children. Remember, the power to bridge the divide lies within your willingness to make the relationship with your child a nonnegotiable priority. This will ensure that you, as their guide, have made an intentional decision to show them how important, valued, and loved they are by you.

We are in this together!

THINGS I WISH MY PARENTS KNEW . . .

I don't want to fight with my mom anymore. I wish she knew how much I love her. I want to be able to tell her things. She's the strongest person I know and I'm thankful for everything she does.

–

Your divorce wasn't just hard on you; it was really hard for me too.

–

I want my parents to know that I know they are not perfect, but there has never been a dull moment where they haven't given me love and everything I need to succeed and pursue my dreams no matter how difficult it may have been.

–

I love you more than anything in existence could begin to describe. I look up to you and I feel indebted to you.

ONE

Love

I was giving a talk one morning in front of about four hundred high school kids. As usual, I had loaded up the car with my guitar and all the sound and lighting equipment I needed for the event. We had every bell and whistle imaginable to make the environment fun, entertaining, and exciting. Regardless of how much I had prepared for that morning, I was not at all ready for what I was about to experience. This day would forever change the way I see the students I speak to.

During the morning's first session, I started by singing a few familiar songs, and as I continued into my talk, I gave it everything I had. This group of teenagers were all in! People were connecting, laughing, and having fun. I was fired up.

And when it came time for a break, a very short, very confident young girl walked up to me. Her name was Marissa.

Despite her small stature, Marissa kind of body-checked me (it was probably more of a push or nudge—a bold move, either way!) out of this massive theater and into a quieter area. "I liked your talk," she said.

"Thank you very much," I responded. "I really appreciate that." I started looking around for my staff because this was getting a little uncomfortable. Marissa was intensely staring at me as if she had something specific to say, and I definitely did not know how this was going to play out.

During the morning's first session, I had shared about the difficult relationship I had with my mom when I was growing up. My mother throughout her life has battled many setbacks, including a long-term prison sentence. When I was a kid, her behavior could be unpredictable. One minute she seemed fine, and the next minute she could turn angry, manipulative, and make me feel that her problems were somehow my fault.

The story I told is always hard to tell, and my feelings about my mother remain complicated to this day. But that morning, the story I told the room just seemed to add fuel to the emotion I was already experiencing. Here is the story I shared:

The setting was in my high school theater, where hundreds of my classmates were gathered to listen to a motivational speaker that was visiting that day. I'll be honest, I couldn't stand motivational speakers. What could this guy say that could actually help me? He didn't even know me. So, as he began his speech, I checked out. Instead of giving this person my attention, I decided to make all my friends sitting around me laugh, which created a distraction as this speaker was trying to deliver his message. I couldn't have cared less. That was until he called me out.

"Hey, funny man."

"Me?"

"Do you think you're funny?"

I quickly thought of a response and replied, "Well, clearly I think I'm funnier than you."

The theater got really quiet, and the speaker asked me to stand up. He continued, "Well, since you obviously don't get the attention that you need at home, and you're demanding all of us give you the attention now, why don't you and I have a conversation? Tell me about your family."

Wow, this guy was good, and before this could get any worse for me, I needed to figure out how to get out of this situation—and fast!

Naturally, I began to speak about someone I was proud of—my dad. I said, "My dad is great. He's fun, funny, he's a musician, and if you knew him, I'm sure you'd like him too."

"I'm sure I would, and you should be thankful that you have a dad that is present in your life, because many in this room do not have that privilege. So, what about your mom?"

I stared back blankly.

I felt extremely embarrassed and insecure and had not even responded yet. I felt like this guy could see right into my soul. He could have taken this moment to make me look like a complete fool, but instead he said, "Your relationship with your mom seems complicated, so I have only one question to ask you. Do you love your mom?"

You could have heard a pin drop in this theater. The tension in the room was almost palatable. As I stood there, feeling completely exposed in front of all my friends, something changed in me. I had never been called out like that before, and as much as I wanted to run out of that theater, I knew I had to stay. This was the first time I didn't care what the people around me thought and was honestly exhausted from pretending I was always okay. For some reason the way this guy asked if I loved my mom, I could tell he genuinely wanted to know. What I said next shocked me. I took a deep breath, looked this speaker in his eyes, and said, "No, sir. I do not love my mom—because how could a mom choose to walk out on her kid?"

His eye contact with me never wavered. He said, "If I can prove to you that you love your mom, will you be willing to sit down and listen to the rest of my talk without distracting the people around you?"

"Give it your best shot."

With kindness and compassion in his voice, he said, "If you didn't love your mom, it wouldn't hurt."

The silence was deafening. Because it did hurt. My mom had made decisions that hurt me—she was doing everything she knew how to survive, even at the cost of breaking my heart. That hurt. I listened to the rest of this guy's speech with a focus that was fierce. What I took away from his talk and the point that, to this day, I share with the students I speak to was his reminder that people, even the ones who love us the most, will not always be perfect or right in how they show their love to us.

Many years later, I found myself still needing to shine a light in the darkness of this relationship, but I didn't know how. My stomach was tight, and I realized I was still holding on to a toxic grudge that I knew I had to set free. Perhaps Marissa had picked up on that as I talked more about this relationship with my mother and how I hoped one day that relationship could be better. Marissa leaned in a bit more and reiterated, "I liked your talk, but you need to do something."

"What do I need to do?"

"You need to call your mom."

I'm not sure why she felt so strongly about this, but my initial instinct was to tell her to go back inside and hang out with her friends until my next session ended, and that we could talk later. Of course, I was also uncomfortable with her request and thinking I would do my best to avoid her.

I tell hundreds, often thousands of teenagers every week to live authentically, face their fears, and love above all else. But it's one thing to talk the talk and quite another to walk the walk. It's relatively easy to say all the right things and get everybody on your side, but it's totally different when that mirror gets turned back toward you. I was being challenged to take a step and call my mom. The timing and place of this rare exchange did not seem ideal, but Marissa (and whatever her reason or feeling she had) was clearly committed to seeing it through to the end.

As parents, I think this happens to all of us from time to time. Kids pick up on the things we like and don't like about ourselves and reflect those attributes back to us. I looked straight into the eyes of this pint-sized girl and said, "Well, I don't know if I have time."

"I think you should make some time."

"Thank you for your courage to find me and thank you for liking my talk. And maybe I'll do that tonight."

"No. You should do it right now."

I had recently built back a bit of a connection with my mom. I did have her number, but I hadn't called her in a while because, to be honest, I didn't think I was ready just yet for the kind of frequent back-and-forth phone call scenario present in many typical parent-child relationships. I had often seen her calls coming in, but I hit the red button much more often than I ever hit the green. I had reached a point where I just didn't want to fight with her anymore, and the only way I knew how to stop the fighting was to turn away from her. I do love my mother, especially when we aren't fighting, and I can only imagine she feels the same.

Marissa insisted. "Call your mom. Now."

Here I was—the expert, the speaker, the person who had been invited to this venue to inspire the audience. On top of that, many students at this event had already written their anonymous letter sharing things they wish their parents knew—with my hope being they would have the courage to share what they wrote about when they got home to their parents. But now the tables had turned, and Marissa was the one who was speaking to me. I was the one not "going home" to talk to my mom about our struggling relationship, about the things bothering me.

I stood there wrestling with potential escape tactics—should I call a different number and pretend that she hadn't picked up? Should I feign a leg cramp and collapse to the floor? No. I knew Marissa wouldn't fall for any of that.

As a public figure, I have long believed in my ability to help others, but I now know that I'm also going to be challenged to take my own medicine. How can I authentically help others if I am not willing to do what I encourage others to consider?

"Practice what you preach" sounded with a new resonance that day.

So I picked up my phone, scrolled through my contacts, and found my mom. Marissa gave me a look that assured me I was not alone.

She simply said, "Go ahead—you've got this."

I pushed my mom's number, and the phone began to ring. I'll be honest with you—I was praying, *Oh, please, please,* please *go to voicemail.* I held the phone up, and Marissa pulled it away from my ear.

"Put it on speakerphone," she said.

Who was this child?

So I put the phone on speaker, and it kept ringing. And then I heard the sweet sound of voicemail. My prayers had been answered, never mind the guilt of having prayed for help to avoid my mother. I shot Marissa a look as if to say, "Well, I guess we tried." But, as you can appreciate, she was not going to let me off that easy.

"Leave a message," Marissa said.

"Right now?"

"Yes, now, and I'd like to hear."

After the voicemail message ended and I heard the beep, I started to speak. "Hey, Mom, it's me. I'm speaking at an event, and I'm here with a friend, and I just wanted to call to see how you're doing. I hope everything's okay. Call me back when you get a chance, and I look forward to talking soon. I hope all is well. I love you."

When I hung up, Marissa thanked me for not being a person who just talks but doesn't take action. In turn, I thanked her for helping me reconnect with my mom. "No problem," she said.

She then disappeared into the crowd, and I never saw her again.

Marissa had called my bluff. It was one of the most moving things someone had done for me in a long time. Marissa, wherever you are, I want you to know that my mom and I have talked a lot more since that day—more than we had in the ten years prior.

You know what's crazy? It took me a very long time to even admit that I loved my mother at all. Until that moment I had worked very hard to build protective walls to seal myself off from any emotion, good, bad, or otherwise, that my mom could inflict on me.

One student said it best in their letter:

> I wish they knew when I seem distant and cold, I need a hug more than ever. I'm not trying to push them away; it's a result of my longing for connection, as backwards as that seems. I wish my parents knew I feel their pain,

> and even when I'm never home, and they don't know what I'm doing, I'm still thinking about them.

Marissa had shown me that I felt my mom's pain, that I was thinking about her even when I didn't call, and the way we express our needs and frustrations toward our parents can be easily misunderstood from the intended desire—such as the need for a hug.

It's the small things that make up the bigger story—in my case, the phone call to my mom. Mother Teresa was known for saying, "We can all do small things with great love." Let's not toss the details aside. When we share the small things with great love, they matter. Include people in your story. Welcome them along for the journey. Don't count on someone like Marissa finding you when you need it most. Instead, *be* a Marissa for the people who need you most. When we commit to consistent personal examination and reflection, we are better able to ask for what we need from the people who are willing and able to help.

EMBRACING ACCOUNTABILITY

Marissa's courage and insight shifted the direction of my life for the better. As someone who has been in front of people their whole life, her words called me to accountability. It was an invitation I could either accept or refuse. I reluctantly accepted, because deep down I knew that my relationship with my mother was affecting every other important relationship in my life: the relationship with my wife, who chose to love me for better or worse; with my kids, who look up to me as their hero; with my team, who count on me to lead authentically; and with my friends, who support and love me beyond my worst mistakes.

Every year, I speak to thousands of students who have more questions than I could ever answer, but I am always committed to sharing something I hope will connect us and potentially allow the moment to turn into a movement for good. As I look out at these faces, curious as to what is coming next, I have learned that to connect, I must be willing to be real. I also accept that although everyone may not fully relate to what I'm about to say, if I share from my heart, most people will be able to take something from the story and apply it in their own life if they choose.

The motivational speaker who asked me if I loved my mother wrecked me. It was the first time in my life I felt that I could not joke my way out of a situation. As a kid, I often used humor to hide behind having to be honest about what I was really feeling or going through. But now, I needed to use self-awareness, empathy, understanding, and compassion—those smaller yet significant ingredients that make up the big picture of love.

CHOOSING LOVE, EVEN WHEN IT HURTS

My relationship with my mom has been hard since the beginning. Her love for me is real, but her own trauma made it difficult for her to provide for me a healthy understanding of love between a mother and son. She had negative relationships with drugs and alcohol and suffered physical and emotional abuse in many of her romantic relationships.

When I was a kid, her behavior was unpredictable. Her way of surviving was to find anything or anyone who could help ease her pain. I had to learn at a very young age how to guard myself from being abused and taken advantage of by the people and situations she exposed me to. She left me under the care and supervision of people who acted inappropriately. One example was when one of her roommates tried to take advantage of me, asking me to lie next to her so she could teach me things that every boy should know how to do. When I became visibly uncomfortable and scared, she immediately made me feel like I had done something wrong. Sternly, she said, "If you say anything, I'll tell your mom what you did. Who do you think she'd believe, me or you?"

I was only six years old. I had no idea what had just happened, but the guilt and disgust I felt toward myself led me into a silence I have carried until writing these words. My mom would have had no clue, and I'm sure if I had told her, she would have done something. But even at that age, the confusion and shame were overwhelming. I believed that speaking up would only get me into trouble.

My mother also made me attend her AA meetings with her, which always made me a bit uncomfortable. I can still remember sitting in the hall of the church where the meeting was taking place, smelling the stench of alcohol in the person's cup next to me. I was only a kid at the time, and I knew this was not a place I should be. This time I stood up for myself and made it clear to my mom that I didn't want to be here and was ready to leave. This clearly created a very uncomfortable situation in the room, but instead of seeing my uncomfortable plea to get out of that place, she brought up an embarrassing secret about me and shared it with everybody in the room.

Ever since I was a kid, I remember being extremely anxious when

I knew my mom and dad would be forced to be together. I don't remember a single time when it was a peaceful encounter between the two of them. It's as if they both knew how to bring out the very worst in each other, and all I wanted was for them to get along. The way I coped with this—by sucking my thumb—and the older I got, the more embarrassing and shameful I felt. And this was the secret she exposed to the room without my consent. With all eyes in the room on my mother and me, she said in front of everyone that I should go to the teenager AA session so I could learn how to stop my thumb-sucking addiction. At this time, I wasn't even close to being a teenager, and the feeling of being exposed to a bunch of strangers was too much to fathom. But I went, and my secret was out, for all to know.

Something changed in me that day. I made a decision to do everything in my power to never be exposed again of anything I felt ashamed of. I began to believe if I made everyone else the center of attention and always redirected the conversation back to them, maybe then no one would ever find out about any embarrassing things about my life.

When I was with my mother, I was around a lot of struggling people and wasn't shown a healthy example of stability. I was always on guard, trying to look like I was good and fine, but inwardly expecting and preparing for something bad that was probably about to happen. Drama and chaos seemed to follow us around. That was my mom.

She used manipulation to try and make sure I saw her as the woman and mother she wanted to be but not the person she actually was. She made everyone else who had any influence on me "bad" so she could be good. She'd tell me my dad was bad and would say things like, "Your dad made me give you up. Your dad beat me up." Things that even back then I knew were too much for any kid to understand.

Things got a lot worse when I was in the second grade. My mom had gotten remarried to a man she'd met from England. We had even moved there for a couple of months. She was willing to do whatever it took to have the picture-perfect image of what a relationship and family was supposed to look like—instead of being honest with herself about what it was. It was a little bit like the way I wasn't being honest when Marissa called me out. It's hard to face the truth sometimes about our relationships.

My mom hit rock bottom when this marriage fell apart, and she had nowhere to go. We moved back to Corpus Christi, Texas, where my Aunt Linda welcomed us into her home. I don't think Linda's husband, Bill, loved the idea, and he was very distant with me. Their kids were already grown, and I'm sure Uncle Bill was looking forward to enjoying a peaceful retirement with his wife. Aunt Linda never spoke a bad word to me about my mom. It was also the first time in my life with my mom that there was a sense of structure and stability. Throughout that year, Aunt Linda was the one who would pick me up from school, take me to appointments, and help me with whatever I needed.

During this time my mom was struggling with her own battles of addiction and did not have the ability to provide the direction and support I needed. I am forever grateful for the sacrifice that Aunt Linda and Uncle Bill made for me during that time, but the situation was not sustainable. That year, my mom got sick and would no longer be able to care for me for the foreseeable future. I was forced to move to Houston to live with my dad full-time. I always loved the time I got to spend with him, though it had only been for the occasional weekend and summers up until that point. This was a change I was actually looking forward to.

I found out later that the only way that my dad would agree to take me in was if he had full custody of me. My mom had no other option but to sign the papers. Looking back, this was the best decision my dad could have made to give me the best opportunity to succeed. He did not have much in terms of material things, but he made the most of what he did have. Our home always had an open-door policy. It didn't matter the time; it didn't matter the reason; you were always a welcome guest in our home. My dad rarely spoke about my mom.

Young Marissa saw what I needed to do and recognized that I needed encouragement and support to do it. Was it difficult? Beyond words. Was it uncomfortable? I wanted to crawl out of my skin! But I did it anyway, with Marissa's help. This girl, who was years and years younger than I was, chose to stand with me. On stage, I am the one who is supposed to have it all together—yet I still needed an ally to stick with me through a difficult moment—a defining moment I didn't even know I desperately needed to walk through until a mirror was held up to reflect my lessons back to me. Marissa, a person I had never met—a total stranger—helped me through this without even knowing how complicated this relationship was.

Since that phone call, I've looked at every student not as someone I talk *to*, but as someone I have the opportunity to journey *with*. As they pour out their hearts during my events, I now have the strength to turn inward and be truthful about the things I still need to work on. No more avoidance. No more hitting the red button when I know I should hit the green. We're all in a process of improvement. We are all still under construction. And love is about learning—learning about others but also about yourself.

Thanks to Marissa, I have found the space to accept who my mom is, even if I don't agree with everything she does. Our kids crave acceptance. We won't always agree with their decisions, but it's not our job to agree. We're here to guide them to make decisions that their future selves will thank them for.

If Marissa were standing with you, how would she call your bluff? What would she see and encourage you to do? Would you be making a phone call, writing a letter, making time for someone who needs you most?

Or perhaps you would be letting them know the specific way that you need them, as one student so plainly expressed in the heartfelt words of her letter: *I mostly wish my dad would be there for me because he doesn't come to any of my dance competitions and sometimes doesn't even show up to my recitals.* Or another, when he wrote, *I wish my dad knew how much little things mean to me, even if they seem like a waste of time to him.* Another student, in an obvious plea for closeness and affirmation, wrote, *I wish you could one day say you love me (you've never done it).* Sometimes the requests are unbelievably simple yet big enough to make a child's dream come true: *I wish you would play video games with me.*

Sometimes we need to be told what it is we are doing wrong or could do better.

And there is no better time to hear it than the present.

Most of us put off doing the things we must face, and we use the excuse of waiting for the "perfect time." Well, today seems like a great time to begin. No more excuses. We will either find a way, or keep making excuses, but we must own whatever decision we choose from this moment forward. Take the time to write your own letter, or ask your child to write to you. Or simply sit down and talk with them.

This may not be easy and at times may be a little awkward, but I promise it will be worth it.

FINAL THOUGHTS

The important thing to keep in mind is that love is at the heart of our parenting journey. That journey can be terrifying! *I may seem awkward and unsure around you,* one student wrote to her parents, *even after all these years, but I love you.*

And your kids *do* love you, even if they have trouble showing it, which they naturally will. They recognize your love for them as well. One student wrote, *I am grateful for what they've done for me, even though I do not show it. I will always love my parents from the bottom of my heart. Sometimes I become distant, but I do love them. I'm just really embarrassed to say I love them, but I do.* Another student wrote, *Even though I can sometimes ignore all the attention and care that has been given to me, I remember all of it.*

Our children do notice our love for them, the things we do for them, and our desire to connect. The purpose of this book is to help make that connection between you and your child stronger. They long for this as much as you do. One student wrote, *I wish my parents knew how badly I want to be able to spend time with them and show them compassion.* Your child may not always have the words to express their need for closeness and affirmation of your love for them, but it is guaranteed they desire it.

As we courageously build a greater connection with our kids, we are making a profitable investment for the future of this relationship. What could be more important than this? This path will not only create more opportunities for deeper conversations but also become a way for us as parents to better ourselves. Please consider the following suggestions and feel free to make them your own.

ACCEPT

A child will not stop loving their parents because of their parents' negative behaviors and actions; they will stop loving themselves.

REFLECT

You are the greatest influence in your child's life. This responsibility is one of the most important and significant gifts that has been entrusted to you. As a parent (guide), how has your influence over this past week helped your kid become a better version of themselves? How has it helped them know and believe they are loved? Do you sense they are looking for love and acceptance in ways that could be unsafe? Does your child feel they are permitted to talk about things even if what they say might disappoint or hurt you?

CONNECT

Set aside time each week to listen and understand what your child wants you to know—start with a minimum of ten minutes a week. Here are a few questions to help you get started:

- What was the best part of your day today? Did everything go smoothly at school, or did anything happen that was not so great?
- What is one thing I can do for you to make your day better?
- Is there something you've been wanting to talk about but haven't found the right time?
- What is something we could do together as a family that you would look forward to?
- How do you feel about your relationships with your friends? Your teachers? How do you feel about our relationship? Is there anything you think I could do better?

Another tip I have found helpful with these conversations is to THINK—that is, ask if it is *t*rue, *h*elpful, *i*nspiring, *n*ecessary, and *k*ind.

No matter what is being talked about, slowing down to consider your words can help strengthen the connection—especially when it takes courage to begin the conversation.

THINGS I WISH MY PARENTS KNEW . . .

I wish you knew that I am getting bullied. I don't feel safe. I don't know what to do.

—

I may not show who I am completely on the inside, but I feel safe at home.

—

If we tell them to "go away" or to "leave me alone" sometimes it's best to barge through the door anyway. We honestly cannot do life alone, and we need them to tell us that everything will be okay. . . . Don't leave us alone. Keep it up until we let you in.

—

I wish my parents knew that sometimes, what they think will help us might actually hurt us. Let us solve problems on our own. Let us experience things on our own. Let us fail and fall down to learn how to succeed and get back up.

TWO

Safety

Everyone, no matter what age, wants to fit in. Fitting in makes us feel safe and wanted, secure that we have a place in the world. The threat of embarrassment, for a kid or teen, can feel downright dangerous. Or at least it did for me.

At the start of my seventh-grade year, my dad decided to change careers. He started a silk-screening business, printing T-shirts for local companies and sports teams. He would come home every day with a new garment that had my name printed on it. He was so proud, and I was so uncomfortable. It wasn't long before practically everything I owned had my name on it. I grinned and bore it when he printed my name on my backpack and my guitar strap, but he stepped over the line when he brought home a T-shirt with my name printed right in the center of my chest and, just below that—I kid you not—our home telephone number.

My dad thought this was the greatest gift he could have given me. If I wore this shirt to school, everyone would know my name, which, he assured me, was a good thing. How desperate would this make me look, though? Seriously, my phone number was the subtitle of my name! What in the world would my friends think? I had a big decision to make. Would I be willing to risk my reputation as a middle school kid to show my dad how thankful I was for the gift he had made me, embarrassing as it might be?

I didn't sleep much that night, but I walked out of my room the next morning wearing that shirt. I still remember the smile on my dad's face. After all he'd done for me, the least I could do was wear that shirt. The decision to leave his previous job as a vice president of a construction company to start his own business had come with a lot of financial sacrifices, including selling his car and purchasing an old beat-up station wagon. He couldn't care less about what other people thought, because for the first time in a long time he was doing something he loved.

I did ask him to drop me off a block away from the school, but he thought it would be great to drive me to the front so he could see everyone's reaction to the masterpiece of his creation. When I got out of that car and my friends saw the shirt, they all started clapping. I looked back at my dad, and the smile he had when he saw me that morning got even bigger. For the rest of that day, everyone was asking where they could get a shirt like that. Maybe that was my dad's plan all along.

THE PUSH AND THE PULL

Our kids are often embarrassed by us. It may at times feel like they want nothing to do with us. This is a totally normal part of growing up, and it is mission critical that we don't take it personally. When kids exercise their independence, they're beginning to discover their autonomy and who they are. In this chapter, I discuss how to know when to keep pushing and when to let kids stand on their own, as well as how to build up their confidence so they have what they need to make decisions that will keep them safe.

Parenting sometimes reminds me of Bubble Wrap. As a kid, I could entertain myself for hours making those little bubbles *pop*! Bubble Wrap is fun, but when it comes to raising our children, people warn us not to "bubble-wrap" them. You know what they mean—let kids fall. Let them make mistakes. Let them learn how to pick themselves up.

While it may be easy enough to give advice to other parents, it can feel far different to swallow the same pill we quickly prescribe to others. It's difficult to watch our kids experience hardship or conflict. Our instinct is to protect, even when we should let them live and learn on their own—even as we remember that while they are still in our care, we are the ones whose voice will have the greatest influence.

Through many letters I have received, this theme is recurring. Kids desire to learn from their mistakes without having the pressure to always get it right the first time. Though we hold high—and at times unreasonable—expectations for our kids, this serves as a good reminder to make sure we are helping them and not crippling them. Of course, being there for them too much is better than the opposite. One student wrote of her absent parents, *I don't tell you what I do or need because you are always too busy with everything else.* Another wrote, *I wish they knew I am actually very lonely and don't feel like I belong anywhere.* A child that cannot communicate their basic needs cannot feel safe. For parents who want to create a safe world for their children, walking the fine line of stepping too far back or being too overbearing is just one of the many challenges.

FAILING FORWARD

I played football in junior high. I was far from the biggest guy on the team, but I had a big mouth and somehow talked myself into playing first-string wide receiver. On game day, as I was suiting up to play, I put on the biggest pads I could find and strutted around the locker room like I was He-Man-strong and pumped to get out there.

On the field, our team huddled up before the first play after the kickoff. That's when I noticed, from the corner of my eye, some guy running down the bleachers with a camera swinging from his neck.

Oh no. That guy was my very own father!

This wasn't good. My junior high insecurities flared up, and my face must have gone beet red at the sight of my dear, enthusiastic old man. Unfortunately for me—a small guy wanting to be seen as tough—he didn't just stop at the edge of the bleachers. He separated from the crowd and walked over to the sidelines! I was sweating, and now panicking, under the weight of my uniform.

I was sure he was going to stop. He *had* to stop.

But no. He ran *onto* the field and slid up to our huddle! On a scale of one to ten, my mortification had hit eleven by the time he squeezed into the huddle with his camera and snapped away.

Well, that was that. I figured my junior high career as an athlete and potential ladies' man was officially obliterated. I yelled, "What are you doing?"

My dad's response? "I'm so proud of you. You're gonna do great."

That was my dad. He loved me, loved football, and was so excited to watch me play. Love for amateur football may sound like a Texas cliché, but it was true.

Our huddle broke, and we set up. Down, set, hut. I was supposed to turn and block whatever charged at me. But when I turned to stop what was coming, I stepped aside as if I had sent the other team a special invite to tackle me. This guy must have been four times my size! I should have asked to see his birth certificate, since he looked like he could have been in college.

As expected, my coach wasn't too pleased that I went rogue and ran in the opposite direction. He screamed, "What's wrong with you?"

"Coach, did you see that guy? He would have killed me!"

Coach didn't seem to have the same respect for my life as I did and yelled at me to get back in the game. Next play—down, set, hut. Guess what? I did the same thing. I didn't block; I just deflected. Coach yanked me out of the game, and I sat on the bench the rest of the season.

If he could have, my dad would have run back onto the field and blocked for me, but it's a blessing he couldn't.

This game was a defining moment in my adolescence. I made a choice that day and, unfortunately, let down my team. Deep down, I wonder what that football season, even high school, would have been like had I made a different choice. What's the worst that could have happened if I had done my part to be there for my team?

Of course, many moments can be scary, both for our kids and for us as parents. But the lessons we allow our kids to learn in times of adversity become the defining moments they will never forget. It must have been painful for my dad to sit and watch me fail out there on the field, but living through that sure made me want to do better in the future, in whatever I tried next. I had to learn that lesson on my own, and that experience was strong enough to remain a reminder for me to this day.

Either intentionally or unintentionally, I believe the reason we overprotect is because we want our kids to be safe—and maybe my dad squeezed his way into that huddle because he was actually a little scared for me, and it was his way of staying nearby. Life experiences have given us wisdom we naturally want to share with our kids so they don't have to make the same mistakes we did. Though this may seem logical and ideal, the reality we must accept is that our kids also need to learn things for themselves. I'm not suggesting that we should let our kids do whatever they want, whenever they want; I'm just asking you to remember what it was like when you were a kid. Some of the most memorable lessons we learned are the ones we learned on our own.

I also played baseball. To be honest, I wasn't very good, but I understood the goal: *Do everything you can to get home safe.* Same goes for our kids—do everything you can to teach them how to get home safe. Without bubble-wrapping them—a tall order!

MAKING HOME A SAFE ZONE

Speaking with parents over the years, I have discovered one interesting thing that happens when some kids come home from school or after spending time with friends. Maybe you've experienced this:

Let's say you go and pick your kid up from one of their friends' homes. The friend's parent answers the door and begins to share with you how amazing your kid is. They explain how your kid set the table, tidied up the living room, and even suggested they could sweep the floor. As your kid stands in the doorway smiling from ear to ear, you do everything you can not to ask if they're sure it's your kid they're *talking about.* You thank them, and on the ride home you are speechless. What the heck just happened? When you get home, your still-smiling kid walks through the front door, throws their jacket, backpack, and shoes anywhere, grabs a snack, walks directly into their room, and slams the door.

What's really going on here? Our kids spend every day discovering new things about themselves while at the same time doing their best to keep up with their friends—all the while knowing that everything they do or say could be recorded and posted on social media. One comment taken out of context or misunderstanding could create weeks of reparation. What may feel like a disconnected, ungrateful kid is actually a kid who has come home to a safe place where they can be themselves and not feel like they must pretend or create a façade. Having shed all the expectations from the outside world, our kids just crave a little space to reconnect with their reality and with themselves. And if you feel something is off with them? Well, once they feel safe, you can use that as a prime opportunity to check in and see how they're doing.

The questions you ask them are critical in terms of their well-being—whether they actually are safe or not. In their responses, you can discover the things that are bothering them, distracting them, and/or exciting them. Even if you ask questions and only get a one- or two-word answer, you've shown them that you care, and even better, are interested and want to know how things are really going. If you find yourself struggling to figure out what questions to ask in fear of a meltdown or an "I am going to tell you what I feel you need to hear so you'll leave me alone" response, start with just sitting with them, allowing your presence to show them you are available. More often than not, they will eventually start to open up. Let them, and when something that is said intrigues you, follow up with "Tell me more." This is a direct and at the same time disarming way for them to know you are really interested and invested in what they are going through.

As I look back at that football game, I realize that my dad was just a proud parent—and maybe he had just a tiny bit of nervous energy. He would have done anything for me. But you know what he couldn't do? He couldn't be on that football field as I watched someone charge toward me. It was my job to stand in that moment, to be the person I was supposed to be. I had to face the truth, even if it meant facing failure.

As parents, we're just as scared as our kids are as they pass through every new experience and cross every new milestone. When I dropped my daughter off for her first day of preschool, I could see the uncertainty in her eyes. And I was scared, too! But we said our goodbyes, and in no time at all she was racing toward the classroom, eager to start her school day.

I was taking a "risk" when I dropped my child off—that she would be okay without me by her side. No matter how big or small, the risks we take as parents also show our children a good example. As one student adeptly put it in their letter to their parents:

> We want to be just as proud of our accomplishments as you are of yours. That if you want to push me to take risks where I may fail, I need to see you take risks where you may fail. I need you to tell me you're proud of my effort, because all my efforts are meant for you. Not my accomplishments, so that I learn to try the things I don't already know I can do.

If we're honest, the Bubble Wrap is often more for us than for our kids. As our kids get older, they become stronger, braver, and hopefully wiser. This also means that some of the risks they take will be greater. It is imperative we understand that we are the greatest influence in our kids' lives and more often than not will be the ones they will come to first, especially when things don't work out the way they planned. While it's sometimes hard for our kids to tell us what they need, or to let us in, they must know that we are there for them and that they are safe with us. When they believe and know they are safe, they will trust that when circumstances or situations feel unsafe outside of the home, home is where they can go to reset, rest, and recharge.

FINAL THOUGHTS

When we find ourselves struggling to know how to support and protect our kids, remember your track record thus far. It is always a good practice to reflect on how things played out in previous circumstances. This is where we as parents can draw from the wisdom of our past to guide our kids through their current situation. You can see in your kids what they cannot yet see in themselves, which is why your guidance, protection, and direction is so important—all while giving them the space and freedom to succeed or fail on their own.

We will not always get this right the first time, just as our kids are learning as they navigate their own experiences. Many of the actions we take as parents have an indirect effect on their overall safety and how safe they will feel and be as adults. Remember, it's the small things that add up to the big picture. When we do things like clearly defining the line between what is accepted and unacceptable in our home and offer them opportunities to do the right thing, we are helping them become responsible and aware as they think through their next decision.

ACCEPT

Perfect parents exist; they just don't have any kids yet.

REFLECT

Once you teach your kids to look both ways, eventually you must let them cross the street on their own. As our kids begin to seek autonomy, their mistakes are not a reflection of you as their parent; they are the lessons that, under your care, allowed them to learn on their own. In what ways can you create more opportunities for your kids to take ownership of their decisions and navigate the outcomes that follow?

CONNECT

When they are scared or apprehensive, let them come to you for insight. Offer your opinion when asked, not only when you feel like it. Here are a few suggestions to help:

- Be approachable and patient, remembering that they may not be able to fully articulate what they are trying to communicate, especially if they feel fearful of being in some kind of trouble.
- Listen to understand—repeat back to them what you heard to show them you are engaged and interested. "Tell me more" is a great option to help them work through what they are trying to say.
- Ask if they would like to hear what you think.
- If the problem/situation is not fixed immediately and they still feel anxious or fearful, that's okay, but always follow up when the time feels right. This will build more trust and encourage them to seek your counsel and guidance more often, knowing that you are there to support and protect them whenever they need it.

THINGS I WISH MY PARENTS KNEW . . .

I love them. But I wish they weren't so controlling, and I wish they understood boundaries. I know they are only trying to love me, but there are so many different ways they could show me. I just feel like they don't have trust in me. I can't always be perfect, but I can handle myself. I need to grow up and experience new things outside of my comfort zone.

—

I wish our parents would lead by example. I see and hear more than they think.

THREE

Guardrails

In September of my eighth-grade year, my mom got remarried and moved closer to where my dad and I lived. I immediately felt the tension of being pulled to spend time with my mom, even though I'd grown comfortable with the safer, more predictable rhythm of life I had with my dad. It was hard for me to understand that my mom was trying her best to rebuild our relationship. Relationships have an interesting way of revealing the good in a person and at the same time drawing out areas in a person that need work and attention.

I think most people want to have good and healthy relationships with their loved ones, but in reality, the work that is required is often more than we feel we can give. I saw this modeled for me in the relationship between my parents as well as with the many men who came in and out of my mom's life. I saw things no child should ever have to see—which included verbal and physical abuse, substance abuse, and infidelity. There weren't enough "guardrails," or boundaries, between my mother's behavior and what I was permitted to witness versus what a child should be shielded from.

My mom married a guy named Ronnie. In the beginning, the relationship was refreshing. It was good, and they were happy. I could tell they had something special, as I hadn't seen my mom happy like that in years. My mother and Ronnie lived in a small apartment about fifteen minutes from my dad's place, so I was able to visit them quite a bit. I had my own room there.

Ronnie was a golfer, so we would often sneak out to the golf course across the street from their place and swing some clubs around. I thought that was really cool. However, things eventually started to change. I noticed the volume of the conversations between my mother and Ronnie increased, and these quickly turned into daily yelling matches.

Initially, Ronnie never lost his cool in front of me, but then his short temper started to come out. I thought, *Whoa, this is not good.* And my mom knew exactly what to say to get him to the point when he would snap. One night in particular, I was in the back seat of their car. My mom was driving, and Ronnie was in the passenger seat when he began to rage. Ronnie was a mechanic, and he was still wearing his work boots. He started stomping his feet on the floor of the car. Then he got to pounding the boots on the dashboard of the car, *boom, boom, boom!* I was scared; I didn't know what to do. I was just trying to kind of hide in the back and be as still as possible. My mom literally drove right up to the police station while Ronnie was in this state. When Ronnie saw where we were, he quickly changed his demeanor as if nothing had happened. The police came out, saw that everything looked calm, and we drove away. The police didn't asked me anything, and they didn't question my mom either. I thought, *This is weird, right?*

On another occasion, I remember playing soccer outside with some friends when a car drove past. I thought, *That looks like Ronnie's car.* And then I saw it parked a short distance away with another woman inside. I could see they were making out in the car, and I didn't know what to do with that information. I didn't want to break my mom's heart, because, as dysfunctional as their marriage was, she still seemed happier than I had ever seen her. So there I was, caught in this place of keeping secrets and knowing too much. What was I supposed to do? I eventually decided to tell my mom. "I think I saw Ronnie in the car with another lady," I told her. But my mom dismissed it, saying, "No, that couldn't have been him." She just wouldn't accept it.

The fact that we were having this conversation at all is testament to the fact that there were not a lot of healthy boundaries in our parent-child relationship.

My mom and Ronnie ended up buying a house that was only a five-minute walk to my junior high, and that's when things got dark. Ronnie was a cocaine addict, and the abuse, both emotional and physical, spun out of control. Any guardrails that had existed in the parenting structure were now nowhere to be found. I remember walking into my mom's bedroom and seeing piles and piles of cash everywhere. I'd never seen money like that before. I asked, "Mom, what is this?" She replied, "I'm taking everything from him. He owes me everything. I gave him my life, and he wants to divorce me? I'm gonna bleed him."

I was like, "Wait, wait, wait a minute. You can't do that." I was a teenager at this point and felt sure that I knew right from wrong, and this was another level of crazy. But my mom took all the money and left town for a while. I can't remember why I was alone in their house, but my mom warned me that if Ronnie came back, she had a restraining order against him and the only thing I had to do was call the police. Well, Ronnie did come back once he found out about the money. He was in a rage. I heard the door slam and I thought, *Oh my God, that's him.* I ran into the closet in my room and hid for I don't know how long. I waited for what seemed like an eternity. I could hear him throwing things around, and I thought, *Oh my goodness, if he finds me, what's he gonna do?* When you're in a state like that, everything's dark, right? Everything's crazy. Thankfully Ronnie didn't find me that day—he was an addict and was most likely high, so who knows what sort of lapse in judgment he would have had.

Shortly after their divorce, my mom warned me not to ever make her choose between a man and me again, because she wasn't sure who she would choose. Those were her exact words. We were in the car when she said that, and I felt a sting. Something precious that exists between parent and child—namely, the way a parent prioritizes their child over everything and everyone else, an often unspoken "boundary" in the parent-child relationship—had been forever violated.

NO BOUNDARIES, NO BALANCE

Ronnie ended up passing away years later. I think that was the last time my mom was stable in my life in terms of just being physically present. She would disappear for months on end after that. I just wanted my mom to be happy, in whatever manner and capacity that happiness was possible for her. I know now that no kid should have to worry about their parents' happiness.

One student summed this up well when they wrote, *I'm only fourteen; I can't fix your problems.* This seems like common sense, doesn't it? But it is important for every parent to truly cross-check themselves on this. Ask yourself, *Are there things I put on my child's plate that I shouldn't?* You may be surprised at what you dig up.

Trying to ensure a parent's happiness is a huge burden to carry. No doubt it was experiences like these that taught me to always lay low. Never look for accolades. Always ride in the back seat, so to speak, because that's the position I felt I was forced into from a young age.

At the age of thirteen, I began searching for ways to numb this pain. I began experimenting with anything and everything that would help the anxiety calm down. I felt lost and directionless. My innocence was fading, my heart was breaking, and I felt I had no one to talk to about it.

The lack of boundaries in the parental relationship I was in caused serious problems. There were no clear rules, and there were no limits on the inappropriate behavior I was being exposed to in my mother and stepfather's personal relationship.

In this chapter, I present a few thoughts and suggestions about boundaries. Let's begin by breaking down what boundaries are. For example, we could replace the word *boundaries* with rules, guidelines, expectations, or even regulations. How we share this information is important, because if you're like me and hear the word *rules*, you immediately start trying to figure out how you can get around them. (I seriously still need to work on this.)

The word that best helps me understand boundaries is *guardrails.* Guardrails protect us from ourselves when we lose control and at the same time protect us from the oncoming traffic when someone on the other side loses control. This visual has been extremely helpful to me as I guide my kids forward. The reason I am so passionate about this is that what many teenagers have shared with me about things they have done and need help understanding are things they feel are not permitted to be talked about.

If teens don't feel comfortable talking about these things, it can make boundary setting (for both the parent and the child) quite difficult. That's why the first chapter is so important; an open loving relationship with regular communication can help make boundaries and rules easier to put in place and, ultimately, to live by.

In theory, following guardrails sounds great and doable. In practice, it takes preparation and an understanding of where you're starting from and where you hope to arrive. Defining the desired destination of what your family hopes to be like in the future is the beginning. Getting clear about this could start by creating a family vision or mission statement.

BITTERSWEET LESSONS

As I mentioned, when I was very little, my mom and I lived in Corpus Christi, Texas. Corpus Christi is on the Gulf of Mexico and is sometimes called the Texas Riviera. It's beautiful and warm with an endless coastline.

This was before Ronnie came along, and my mother was interested in creating normalcy and the healthy guardrails that come along with it.

One day, my mom asked me if I wanted to go fishing. Now, I love fishing, but I typically went with my dad's side of the family. I honestly didn't even know my mom knew how to work a fishing pole, and I was excited to see her doing just that. The plan was to go out to the boat docks and throw a few lines over the edge of the pier. This was going to be great.

The first stop was the grocery store to pick up snacks for our outing. We got some chips and pop and made our way over to the checkout. The checkout counter is what dreams are made of when you're a kid. That's where the candy lives, and where a lot of negotiating happens between kids and their parents. On this fishing trip day, I eyed a lollipop that I just had to have.

"No, Michael," said my mom. "Not today."

I didn't like that answer. Not at all. So, when she wasn't looking, I snagged two of them and hid them in my pocket. On the car ride out to the pier, I reached into my pocket, took out the lollipop, and tore off the wrapper. It tasted amazing. Perfect. Unfortunately, that's when my mom looked over from the driver's seat.

"What is that?" she asked. (She knew exactly what it was.)

"It's a lollipop."

"Where'd you get it?" (She knew exactly where I had gotten it.)

"The store."

"Did you pay for it?" (She knew the answer to this one, too.)

"Pay for it?"

I was young, but my mom knew that even I wasn't that dumb. She pulled the car over and asked why I had taken it.

"I dunno. 'Cause. But look, I got one for you too." (This did not help my case.)

"Just because you want something doesn't mean you can have it, and it doesn't mean you can just take what isn't yours and not pay for it. Give it to me."

I didn't move. Or give it up.

Her voice dropped an octave, and in that "scary mom voice," she said, "Give me . . . the lollipop." Since I preferred to live through the day, I reluctantly handed it over.

She reached into the back seat and retrieved a small paper bag. I opened it and saw five of those very same lollipops inside.

"When you weren't looking, I grabbed a few at the checkout and asked for a little brown bag to hide them in. I wanted to surprise you out at the pier. I want you to have everything in life, but sometimes you have to wait. You must learn how to be patient."

I sensed that this little speech was something I should pay attention to, but all I wanted were the lollipops.

"Okay. Can I have my lollipops?"

"Actually, no. And we're not going fishing either. We've got to go back to the grocery store so you can tell the manager what happened."

Panic washed over me. I didn't want to go to kid jail! It was just a lollipop! My life was over before it had even begun.

Back at the store, I walked up to the store manager, meekly holding the lollipop that I hadn't finished, and attempted to get his attention.

"Um, I took this lollipop without paying for it."

The store manager looked at my mom and just mumbled something like don't worry about it. But my mom said that it wasn't okay, that I needed to apologize properly. So the store manager played along and said, "Okay, I see. Son, you took from this store . . ." and proceeded with a long speech about how stealing takes away from all the hardworking employees and so on. He was a nice guy, but I would have rather been out to sea all alone on a raft than stay in that store one minute longer.

My mom paid for the candy, and I had to go home and do some chores to pay her back. Learning important life lessons is sometimes painful! Even though that wasn't the best day of my life, I remember it vividly because it taught me a few things:

1. Don't steal. (Good to know!)
2. Sometimes the things we want aren't necessarily the things we need right now, or ever.
3. Our actions matter and they have consequences.

This lesson my mom instilled in me still resonates. How easy is it to buy something we don't need, can't afford, or is simply not good for us just because we want the instant gratification? It's hard to hear no in a winner-takes-all sort of environment. And it's difficult as a parent to say no, even if it's for our kids' own good or for a surprise down the line.

My mom wanted me to consider my decisions and to feel the consequences of those decisions whether they were good or bad.

We should teach our kids to pause and consider that even though they desperately want this one *thing*, it might not be what's best for them. Impulse control is hard. And not very fun. But helping them develop self-control and learn the difference between needs and wants is a solid step in the right direction—it teaches them to create boundaries for themselves.

It's okay to let our kids feel the weight of their actions. We want kids to realize they matter and that the choices they make affect those around them. My mom didn't let me off easy with the lollipop incident. She could have told me not to do it again and continued driving, but she didn't. I had to walk through the process of thinking about my actions and working through their consequences.

DEFINE THE LINE

Whenever we start a thought with "one day," it's often a way of expressing a hope or a wish. It's rarely the starting point of action, but more of a vague notion of something we'd like to see happen in the future. It's a place where dreams are stored, where possibilities live, but it's not always where the best decisions are made.

For me, many of my "one day" moments as a kid revolved around the frustration I felt toward my parents. Whether it was my mom telling me to clean my room, my dad saying I couldn't go to my friend's house, or the frequent command to eat my vegetables, one day, I would escape all this!

Of course, these moments of frustration and rebellion mostly took place in my mind. I would craft long, dramatic speeches in my head, filled with all the things I wanted to say but never have the courage to speak aloud. Those speeches were bold, filled with righteous vigor, and full of the certainty that I knew better. But I knew better than to actually say them to my parents—that would have been disastrous.

Those silent, imagined speeches were my coping mechanism—a way to deal with feeling powerless in situations where I had no real control. In those moments, I believed I knew what was best for me, and it felt as if my parents were just getting in the way. It was frustrating, and yet it's an understandable experience for many kids. Children often think they know everything, that their perspective is the only valid one, but in reality, they are blind to the bigger picture they see and live through every day.

Still, there are times when these "one day" ideals turn into "day one" decisions—when something inside shifts and what was once just a vague hope or desire becomes possible.

I had one of those moments one summer afternoon in Texas.

I was sitting in the living room with my dad, clearly bored. Now, as a kid, there was nothing worse than boredom, and in my mind, the solution to boredom was to go outside and play. But I knew better than to tell my dad I was bored. That would've led to him giving me a "suggestion," which usually involved doing something I wasn't interested in. Nine times out of ten, that suggestion was related to chores—things I had been avoiding for as long as possible. So instead of telling him how I felt, I decided to take matters into my own hands and head outside.

As I was about to leave, my dad stopped me and asked where I was going.

"Outside—I need to clear my head."

"That's great, have fun," he said. "But don't go in the street."

I was already halfway out the door when his words stopped me cold. Don't go in the street?

That was all I heard. Suddenly, my excitement about going outside was replaced with frustration. Why did he have to say that? Couldn't he see that the street was the best place to have fun?

My frustration quickly grew into something bigger, and all I could think about was what I couldn't do.

It's strange how boundaries work. When someone tells us not

to do something, it's like everything else fades away, and all we can think about is the one thing we've been forbidden from doing. In my case, I had an entire front yard to play in. There was also the backyard, which was big enough for any number of games. Heck, I could've even gone to my friend Becky's house if I wanted to. But none of that mattered. The only thing I cared about was the one thing I wasn't allowed to do—play in the street.

So I did what any kid would do. I sat down at the edge of the grass, right at the boundary between the yard and the street. I sat there, staring at the asphalt as if it were the most tempting thing in the world. For a while, I just sat, letting my frustration simmer, battling with how serious my dad really was with his command. Eventually, I couldn't resist any longer. I looked back at the house to make sure my dad wasn't watching. Then, cautiously, I stuck my left foot out onto the street. My heart was pounding in my chest as I made contact with the forbidden asphalt. It felt exhilarating—like I was doing something dangerous and rebellious, something thrilling. For that brief moment, I felt powerful. I had crossed the line, and nothing had happened. I hadn't been caught. I hadn't been punished.

But after a few seconds, reality began to set in. I quickly pulled my foot back onto the grass, trying to act as if nothing had happened. I began pacing along the edge of the yard, walking back and forth, trying to decide what to do next. But the pull of the street was still there, stronger than ever. I had already tested the boundary and survived, so why not push it a little further?

Well, as was my typical commitment when I made a decision, I went all in. One foot, then both. Before I knew it, I was standing in the middle of the street, my heart racing with adrenaline. And then

I took it a step further. I lay down in the middle of the street! I was stretched out with my eyes staring up at the clear, blue sky. The sun was shining, and for a moment, I felt like I had won. I had proven to myself I was right in thinking the street was an amazing place, and it felt incredible.

My victory, however, was short-lived. "Michael!" my dad shouted. "Get over here!"

Instant panic set in. My heart leaped into my throat, and I scrambled to my feet. There was no way I could face him now; I had no idea what to do. So I did the only thing that made sense to me in that moment—I ran. I bolted around the back of the house, racing as fast as I could, and slipped in through the back door. I figured this was the closest way to get to my room. Decision made—I made it to my room, slammed the door shut, and leaned against it, trying to catch my breath.

What had I done?

My mind was racing, trying to come up with a plan. I knew I was in trouble. There was no getting around that. But how was I going to face my dad after this? How could I explain what I had done? I was scared, and I didn't know what to do. I had little time before I had to face the consequences, and in that time, I needed to come up with a plan. I decided the best course of action was to run away. I couldn't live like this anymore. I couldn't deal with these unfair rules, these constant limitations. Clearly my dad didn't understand me, and I was done.

I found an old bag in my closet and started packing. Of course, I didn't pack any clothes or essentials. I was a kid, after all. What I packed were the things that mattered most to me at that time—my toys. I crammed as many as I could into the bag, stuffing it to the point where the zipper was on the verge of exploding. But I didn't care. I was leaving, and that was all that mattered to me.

With my bag packed and my mind made up, I took a deep breath and opened my bedroom door. I walked into the living room, where my dad was still sitting on the couch, sipping his ice-filled cup of Coke. He glanced at me as I entered the room but didn't say anything. To him, it seemed like nothing out of the ordinary had happened. But to me, this was a really big deal.

I walked over to the recliner near the front door, dragging my overstuffed bag of essential toys behind me.

My dad finally looked up from his drink and said, "Hey, Michael, what's going on?"

I couldn't believe how casual he was. Didn't he realize that I was about to run away? This was serious! So, with all the confidence I could put together, I looked him in the eye and said, "Dad, I'm leaving. I'm running away."

My dad raised an eyebrow. "Oh?" he said. "Is that so?"

I nodded. "I've already packed my bag. This is it. I'm leaving."

I expected him to try to stop me, to tell me how sorry he was, or maybe even to beg me to stay. I had imagined this moment playing out like a scene from a movie, with dramatic music in the background and heartfelt dialogue. But instead, my dad just shrugged and said, "Well, Michael, I hope you have a great life." He looked at the door, as if to give me permission to leave, and then took another sip of his Coke.

I stood there, stunned. This wasn't how it was supposed to play. But I was stubborn, so I had no other choice but to follow through.

I grabbed my bag and walked out the door, determined to start my new life.

As I reached the edge of the yard, I stopped and looked around. That's when it hit me: I had no plan. I had no idea where I was going or what I was going to do. I didn't have any money, I didn't have any clothes, and I didn't know where I would go. All I had were a few toys stuffed into a bag.

And then I saw it—Jimmy's house. Jimmy was my good friend and lived just across the street. Suddenly, a new plan formed in my mind. I would go to Jimmy's house. I could stay there, and we could live together as brothers. Surely Jimmy's family would take me in, and everything would be fine. I picked up my bag and marched across the street to Jimmy's house. I knocked on the door, and when Jimmy answered, I filled him in so we were on the same page.

"Jimmy," I said, "I've run away from home. I've decided to leave my dad's place, and I'm going to live with you from now on."

Jimmy's face lit up with excitement. "This is the best idea ever!" he shouted.

We went straight to his room and began rearranging things to make space for me. I told him that if my dad came looking for me, we had to pretend I wasn't there. Jimmy agreed, and for a few moments, everything was working just as I had planned.

But then, there was a knock on the door that sent both Jimmy and me into an unexpected panic. I knew it was my dad just by the knock. My heart started racing again. What was I going to do? I couldn't face him now, not after everything that I had done. So I did the only thing I could think of—I hid. I crawled under Jimmy's bed and told him that we were now brothers, and he couldn't tell my dad I was here.

Jimmy opened the door, and seeing my dad standing there, he said, "Hi, Mr. Billy. What can I do for you?"

"Jimmy," my dad replied, "I'm looking for my son. I saw him walk over here with his bag, and I know he's here. I will only give you one chance to do the right thing, so, Jimmy, I need you to tell me where he is."

For a brief moment, I thought Jimmy would try to stall to buy both of us a little more time. But without missing a beat, Jimmy pointed to the bed and said, "Mr. Billy, Michael is under my bed."

I was caught. I knew I was in trouble now, and there was no way out of it.

My dad didn't say a word as he walked into the room, reached under the bed, and grabbed my ear. He marched me out of the house by my ear and across the street to our home. I tried to plead that this was child abuse, but he was very clear that this was parenting. (To be clear, I was safe, unharmed, and in competent care.)

When we got home, my dad sat me down at the kitchen table. I could feel my heart beating out of my chest as I waited for him to speak. Finally, he asked, "Why did you think it was a good idea to run away?"

I hesitated, trying to come up with a worthy explanation.

"I was mad," I finally said. "You wouldn't let me play in the street."

My dad sighed. I could tell he was trying not to smile, but he was also taking my feelings seriously.

"Do you know why I told you not to play in the street?" he asked.

I shrugged. "No."

"Do you remember what happened a few months ago when you were visiting your mom?" he asked. "Do you remember the phone call I got?"

I shook my head. "Not really."

My dad took a deep breath and told me the story. He explained how, a few months earlier, when I was staying with my mom, I had been hit by a car. I had been playing outside, and when my mom asked me to get in the car, I had raced out into the street without looking. That was when the car hit me. Thankfully, the accident wasn't serious, and I only had a few scrapes and bruises. But my dad had received a call from the hospital, telling him what had happened. In that moment, I can only imagine what was going through his head. He hadn't known the extent of my injuries, and he was scared that something terrible had happened to me.

As my dad told me this story, I could see the emotion in his eyes, and his shaky voice only made the moment more intense. This wasn't about rules for the sake of rules. This was about love. He had told me not to play in the street because he couldn't bear the thought of losing me.

I pieced together his recent experience of the call he received that his son had been in an accident, without context or details, and couldn't imagine going through that again. In that moment, I understood why my dad had set that boundary. Though I didn't like it or understand why, I realized he wasn't trying to ruin my fun; he was only trying to protect me.

I apologized for running away, and I expected that would be the end of that. But of course, there were consequences. I was grounded for a week, which at the time felt like an eternity. Looking back now, I realize that being grounded wasn't just about punishment, it was about learning to accept my dad's guidance. It was about understanding that he set rules for a reason, even if I didn't always agree or understand them.

As kids, we often think we know what's best for ourselves, but we don't always see the bigger picture. We think our parents are just being strict or unfair, but in reality, they are doing their best to keep us safe and guide us in the right direction. It's only when we grow older that we begin to understand the wisdom behind their decisions.

If you're struggling with how to set boundaries with your kids, let them know that *no for now does not mean no forever.* What we're learning from the letters is that kids want and need to understand *why* we say no. We may not have a good explanation every time something comes up, but what if we explained the *why* more than responding with "Because I said so"? When our kids trust us to guide them, they can then trust that we consistently have their best interest in mind. On the flip side, if our kids rarely understand the reason of our decision, especially when it personally affects them, the connection in that relationship will lose its strength over time.

Failing to explain *why* we say no is perhaps the reason so many of our kids push us to a point of frustration after we have laid down the law over one thing or another. Of course, we cannot always explain in detail the reason, but being mindful of the times that we can (and should) will go a long way in your future relationship with them.

—

When I talk about my mom, I often refer to the struggles I've had to face with her over the years. But the truth is that she was also a very wise woman who loved me the best she could, and I am grateful for the lessons I learned from her.

However—and I'll emphasize again and again that we are all a work in process—my mom missed the mark in one key area: She never sought to understand *why* I stole the lollipop in the first place (other than the obvious things like it was delicious and most kids love candy). If she had asked, really asked, she would have discovered that I was nervous on the days I went out with her. She loved me, but she was not always a stable presence in my life. I developed my own coping behaviors to deal with the anxiety I often felt when I spent time with her. I now look back on that day and see that the lollipop was just another distraction for me.

Now, I know there is no way I could have verbalized all that at the time, and even if I had, perhaps my mom would have played down whatever I said about how her behaviors could make me feel because that would have been a hard truth to hear—but I reflect on that incident now and hope to do better with my kids and seek to understand why *they* sometimes do things that anger or disappoint me.

True understanding works both ways. This invites us to authentically desire and pursue to understand what is going on with our kids—why they go over the guardrails and push boundaries we have set for them. Most likely they will not be able to articulate it perfectly, but as they begin to open up, let them struggle through the words and repeat back to them what you hear. Allow them to correct or change whatever they need so they will feel heard and understood. We cannot defeat what we cannot define.

I want to encourage you to help your kids understand *why*. They may not like it, they will question it, and at times they will rebel against it, but teaching them that setting reasonable guardrails is necessary to get the most out of life will provide practical tools from real-life experience to guide their decision-making in the future.

FINAL THOUGHTS

Boundaries, or guardrails, need to be seen and understood. We cannot expect our kids to always know what's right and wrong. Guardrails help our kids understand that feelings do not always mean truth. Just because I feel that driving on the opposite side of the road would get me to my destination faster doesn't mean I should do it. You are their parent, not their friend—and you are so much more than this. Your willingness to be the parent now will make the relationship with your kids in the future better than a friendship—it will have a connection that will never lose the signal, even beyond the grave.

Consider defining guardrails around areas like:

- Family time
- Mealtime
- Friends/social time
- Technology
- Bedtime
- Homework

ACCEPT

When we teach our children that *no* is a complete sentence, it gives them permission to discover and protect their value and worth.

REFLECT

Saying no to our kids can sometimes be a challenging task. As our kids get older and are exposed to new people and experiences, creating guardrails to protect them is critically important. Ultimately, saying no to certain things allows us the ability to honor the commitments we have already said yes to.

CONNECT

If everything is important, nothing is important. Take stock of how many things your child is involved in and support them in creating boundaries around what is most important for them to continue with.

Here are a few suggestions to help:

- Saying no for now does not mean it will be no forever.
- Helping your kid learn decision-making skills is a master class you are equipped to teach. Share an experience in which a boundary set by your parents was hard for you to accept but that you now are grateful for.
- Ask your child if there is a rule or boundary they are struggling with and why. Help them understand why the boundary is in place, and be clear about the consequences for not following any given rule. This sets the guardrails in place with clarity and understanding.

THINGS I WISH MY PARENTS KNEW . . .

All I want is their support, but often I feel criticized instead.

—

The reason I haven't told them the truth is because I don't want to disappoint them, and I don't want them to feel like they have failed as parents.

—

I am trying my best. Your job is to make sure that I feel good enough and to show me that what I do is appreciated; tearing me down does not motivate me to be better.

FOUR

Guidance

Have you ever attempted to get away with something and failed miserably? One of the earliest memories I have of suffering through this questionable behavior was back in the third grade. Third grade was a tough year for me. That was the year I moved in full-time with my dad and changed schools. I was suddenly the new kid at school, and nobody knew me. It all felt a bit terrifying. When I arrived, I got placed into the International Baccalaureate (IB) program focused on developing intellectual, emotional, personal, and social skills. This class felt really hard for me. I was always the guy who couldn't focus in school, and my mind was often someplace else.

I received a bad grade on some homework and my teacher, Mrs. LeCour—I'll always remember her name—came up to me and said, "You need to take this assignment home and get your dad to sign it."

I can assure you I did not like the sound of this whatsoever.

"This is going to be a good thing, because you're going to show your dad that you need some support. And maybe your dad can help you with some of the issues in school, and he can sit down with you and show you."

I thought, *You're the teacher. I think you're the one who should show me, and we don't need to involve my dad.* But what I said out loud was, "I'm okay, ma'am. My dad won't want to see that, so how about I promise to do my work next time."

Of course, I lost this battle with Mrs. LeCour and was sent home with a piece of paper to be signed by my father that evening. I may not have always paid attention in class, but I was good at scheming for creative ways to get out of trouble. I was only eight years old, but even I knew that adults tended to sign important-looking things in cursive, those strange scrawling letters that all flowed mysteriously together.

Did you ever have those banners posted across the walls of your elementary-school classroom that showed the letters in uppercase, lowercase, and cursive? That's what we had in Mrs. LeCour's class. I looked up and saw those cursive letters, written perfectly, and got a genius idea. What if I just practiced my dad's name in those cursive letters and wrote his signature for him? I could save him some time and he wouldn't have to be bothered by my little problem!

I spent the last half of class trying to write *B-i-l-l-y C-h-i-a-s-s-o-n* in those lovely flowing letters. That night I practiced some more, and I got it down to where I thought my dad's name looked really convincing in beautiful cursive writing. Then I took out that slip from the teacher and signed it *Billy Chiasson.* I was so proud and positive that everything was going to be fine. Isn't it funny that when pressured by time to learn something new, we can usually find the drive to get it done?

I showed up at school the next morning feeling confident. I just sat at my desk waiting for Mrs. LeCour to ask me what I knew she was going to ask me.

"Mr. Chiasson, do you have something for me?"

"Yes, ma'am."

I reached into my desk, pulled out that piece of paper, handed it to her, and said, "There you go."

She looked at the paper and silently walked back to her desk.

She said nothing. I had gotten away with it! *Man, I could conquer anything!* Sure, a thought deep down also tugged at me, because I knew I had done something wrong.

At recess, Mrs. LeCour pulled me aside. "Can I talk to you? Did your dad sign that piece of paper?"

"Yep."

"Michael, did your dad sign that paper?"

I remained silent, but my traitorous face revealed the truth. I knew I was caught.

"Why do you think I asked you to bring that home to get your dad to sign it?"

"Because I didn't do my homework."

She asked me if I understood why it was important that my dad knew about my schoolwork. I honestly did not know and told her exactly that. She assured me that I was obviously a funny, talented kid, but she also made it clear that one way or another, she was going to tell my dad about my failed assignment—and my failed prank.

She wrote a new letter to my father and instructed me not to read it. This time, I knew better than to disobey. I gave the letter to my dad that night. He read it and laughed.

"Are you kidding me?" he said. "I don't even write like that! Michael, even if I get mad, it doesn't change that I love you. I'm your dad. I'm here for you."

Now, the interesting part about this story is that my teacher, my guide, corrected me privately. Had she announced it to the class, she would have crippled me. Her guidance throughout this process paved a way for me to build a stronger relationship with my dad, which became a gift that I will forever be thankful for.

DISCOVERING YOUR TRIBE

One student, in their letter to their parents, wrote, *I wish they knew how I feel embarrassed when I'm corrected in front of others.* My teacher never did that, and it made a world of difference in my ability to better myself that she didn't.

With that, I take a moment to acknowledge and thank all the incredible teachers who spend countless hours every year helping our kids navigate through some of the most challenging years of their lives—and do so discreetly, involving parents and other academic staff only when needed. What continually amazes me about Mrs. LeCour is that she was experienced enough to know that my father had to be brought into the conversation. And when he was, he was able to provide the right support I needed. She didn't scold or shame me, either.

Many children and teens are not given this kind of support. In one letter, a student wrote of their own experience:

> I can control my emotions in front of others, but I wish they knew how emotionally unstable I am. I have feelings, and I also get hurt whenever they call me names. I wish they knew that I distance myself from them because all they do is point out my flaws. Some words really sting. I am trying hard to make them

> proud and be a good daughter, but they just don't see that. I also need appreciation from them sometimes. I wish they would stop comparing me to others because I am not them. I am different from them. I wish they would stop thinking I'm just like their rebel teenager selves. I AM ME, and I love who I am.

When we criticize with careless judgment, it is often a reflection of our need to control. When we offer constructive feedback and guidance with careful judgment, we can incite change. This process of teaching, learning, and unlearning is a lifelong process.

Our kids do want us to notice what they are doing and rein them in when we notice they are taking on unhealthy behaviors. Guidance is desired by them, even welcome! *I wish my parents knew the things I really do on social media,* one student wrote in her letter to her parents. Another admitted, *I wish my parents knew that I need a break from my phone.* Yet another said, *I wish my parents knew that I secretly rebel so I feel like I have control over my life.*

Sometimes our children are screaming to be seen.

Do you remember the game hide-and-go-seek? I played that as a kid, and if I say so myself, I was ridiculously good at it. In one particular game when the whole neighborhood was involved, I found a camouflaged spot between a house and some shrubs. It was well-hidden but still pretty close by. I was crouched down hiding for what seemed like an eternity before I noticed I couldn't hear people running around and screaming anymore. Finally, I moved out of the place where I'd been hiding with my arms up as if I'd won the title of world champion hide-and-go-seek master. There was no one in sight. My first thought was that maybe we were all still playing. But then I heard music and laughing in a friend's backyard. When I arrived there, everyone was like, "Hey, Michael, where were you?" Where was I? I had been hiding for what seemed like hours! They said, "Oh yeah, sorry about that." They had quit playing and decided to just hang out.

I laughed off that moment, but if I'm honest, deep down something bothered me. I had been forgotten. No one likes to be forgotten, and what can be also hard and scary for many of us, including our kids, is actually being found. Part of being well-guided and supported involves knowing that you are not alone, that people are there for you and won't abandon you.

One of the greatest desires we all have is to be found—to be seen. We all have things that remain hidden. And it's really hard to reveal those things if we feel that what the other person sees may cause them to think less of us, or at the extreme, reject us. The internal questions of "What will others think?" or "Will I measure up to their expectation?" can be overwhelming.

One of my greatest fears for many years was the fear of being found out. Though I was good at pretending to always have it together on the outside, it was exhausting. I was scared to let anyone fully know me, which made it impossible for me to be fully loved, and not wanting to share my bad grade with my father fit the established pattern. For most of my life, I would be for others what I felt they needed me to be for them. This was a losing game. If you can at all relate to this, you are not alone, and I want to encourage you by rediscovering the good parts of you that have been hidden.

Something that was very helpful for me was to take an audit of all the people in my life, particularly those who had close access to me and who I'd consider more than an acquaintance. I took a piece of paper and wrote down every person's name I could think of, and I answered these questions:

1. Can I tell this person anything and know they would keep that information to themselves? Are they a discreet guide?
2. Can I ask this person for help or advice, and do I believe they would be willing to do whatever they could to help me?
3. Has this person been willing/able to ask me for help?
4. How has this person shaped and guided me through past decisions and how did it turn out?

This process has helped me to deepen the relationships with the people I could trust and create some separation with those I needed to love from a distance. It has helped me determine to whom I should look for guidance and support. The greatest relationship that benefited from this process was with my wife. I discovered that together we are so much stronger and effective. Melissa's intuition and direction for me and our family is something I will never take for granted.

The list is a very valuable one to teach your children, as they select the people who will be their mentors, their true friends, and those who should have limited access to what is shared and talked about.

In the meantime, you are still your child's ultimate guide in life—and that is quite a balancing act. Our kids want us to seek them out and ask questions, and at the same time, they don't want to disappoint us. When we ask questions they are not ready to answer, don't feel the need to push them. Our presence may be all they need in that moment. We don't always have to provide the answers. Our kids are more capable than we sometimes think, and helping them discover that is a great gift.

GUIDE WITH GRACE

While writing this chapter, I was confronted with a thought that unsettled me. The thought came in the form of a question: Do my kids see me as their biggest supporter or their loudest critic? The honest answer to that question was hard to accept.

My son, Simon, is by far the most aware and considerate person I've ever had the privilege of knowing. His deep desire to make sure the people he loves always feel and see that love is inspiring. At his current age, my role in his life is to guide that incredible love he gives so freely to a place where he can also receive the same gift in return. And this is where the answer to that question became difficult to acknowledge.

Simon's outward expression has always been full of life and joy. He can sing like an angel at the top of his lungs while doing a perfect cartwheel, landing with both fists reaching victoriously to the sky. What is innocent, joyful, and visibly fun for him, I sometimes have found to be overwhelming, especially in public. I've caught myself fearing what others might think. Out of my own insecurity, this has led me to correct him in public, which was not only embarrassing but most likely confusing for him. I was not being a good guide, and I am sure I broke our trust in that moment. For that I am deeply sorry.

Everything Simon has ever liked he has pursued with an all-in attitude. I used to think, *If he keeps going with the Lego sets, Disney character collections, gymnastics mats, slime-making kits, books, and toys, our house will soon resemble a full-blown toy store.* Yet here I was, placing the opinions of total strangers above my powerful, brave, and curious son, who was simply discovering what he loved and learning how to make it his own.

What my son has taught me through all of this is how willing he is to be curious, free, and fully committed to discovering his passion and joy, and this has challenged me not to fear outcomes that are different from what I imagined or expected. This has helped me guide him with a lighter hand, carefully weighing when I should correct him and when I should let him be himself and learn how to navigate and discover what he is drawn to that brings him joy and helps build his confidence.

FINAL THOUGHTS

As parents, we have the ability to see in our children what they cannot yet see in themselves. It's also our responsibility to define and uphold a clear image of what is right and acceptable according to our family values, while giving our children the freedom to be curious and ask questions. This allows them to explore who they are within the guardrails we set as their parents. This is important for our kids, as it will build a confidence in them to do amazing things. As we help them make a course correction when they drift beyond our comfort zone, they can receive the guidance as we share it with clarity and grace. Some healthy things to remember as we do this:

- Our role as their parent is and forever will be so much more than just a friend.

- We will not always get it right, but we must never question our ability to make it right.
- Our kids' reactions do not have the same filter with us as they do with others.
- A child is not a problem to be solved, but a person to be known.
- When they push us away, it does not mean they don't love us; they simply may not know how to articulate or express what they need.
- Though our parents were not perfect, we have learned so much from them that has helped us become better parents for our kids.

As parents, we must be mindful of our children's age and what is age-appropriate versus what may be too soon to allow them to do. Likewise, we should be aware of things we have been putting off—things that, if not confronted, will only cause greater tension in the days to come. The point of all of this is for our kids to discover and know for themselves how amazing and capable they really are without feeling the pressure to be a certain version of themselves when they are with us versus the honest and real version of who they feel they are around everyone else.

ACCEPT

What we say, what we do, and how we respond all shape our child's value and character.

REFLECT

Part of guiding well is to live by what we say and admit when we haven't. This lesson is a leader's superpower. When we show our kids that we have the humility to own our mistakes, we model integrity. If we parent from a "do as I say and not as I do" model, we undermine the values we aim to instill in them. We lose our kids' trust. From the beginning, our kids learn from observation, which is then naturally followed by imitation. As we strive to live the values we hope to see in our kids, this becomes a powerful and authentic blueprint that models how it is done.

CONNECT

Share with your child something they were right about that taught you something new. Here are a few suggestions to help:

- Express gratitude—if your kid has taught you something, tell them how much you appreciate and needed that. Not only will it boost their confidence, but it will also encourage more conversations and connections like this.
- Acknowledge and apologize for a time when you missed the mark.
- Ask your kid if there is something you have done that made them feel hurt or embarrassed—then listen, try not to fix it right away, and thank them for sharing this with you.
- Our kids have an innocent wisdom that can provide answers with clarity and insight. Don't be afraid to ask what they would do in your situation. (Use good judgment with this one!)

THINGS I WISH MY PARENTS KNEW . . .

I wish my parents knew how grateful I am for supporting the decisions I've made, even if it wasn't something they've planned for me to do.

—

I wish my past actions and mistakes didn't change how you see me, because I would have told you what I was doing if I wasn't afraid I'd be punished for it.

—

Despite any differences in our beliefs and values, I still love them. Even when my choices go against their wishes, choosing my own path is not intended to be disrespectful. I must learn my own truth in life. I ask for guidance, not judgment. I also wish they knew that I crave respect for my decisions and lifestyle the same way children are expected to respect parents. Today's pressures are different and so must be our lifestyles.

—

I want them to know that they are the biggest influences in my life, and I wouldn't be where I am today without their encouragement and support.

FIVE

Modeling

After a challenging school year, I took home my final report card and placed the unopened envelope on the table. My dad was never one to make a big deal about getting good grades as long as I was willing to give my best. This particular year, however, was not my best. When he opened my report card, his face said it all. "Michael," he said in a low, slow voice. I'd thought this year couldn't get any worse, but there it was—I had failed the seventh grade.

I tried not to show what I was really feeling, but I was rattled. What would other people think? But above all, what did my dad think?

This was the day I picked up a label that shaped how I saw myself for a long time—*failure*. Most people who knew me would never know this was my belief. On the outside, I could pretend my way through just about anything.

That summer, a friend invited me to attend a special youth event at their church. To be honest, I had no desire to go, but my friend wouldn't take no for an answer. So there I was, sitting in the back corner of the church, counting the minutes until I could leave and do something more fun.

As I sat there, one of the youth ministers spotted me. I did my best to avoid making eye contact, hoping he'd pass me by. No such luck. He made his way over and sat right next to me.

"What's your name?" he asked, with an inviting smile, followed by the ever predictable "How are you doing?"

Like most teenagers trying to avoid a real conversation, I gave the standard go-to response: "I'm good. Everything's fine."

But he didn't buy it. He saw right through my defenses. You could tell that this guy genuinely cared. He didn't settle for the surface-level answers and instead dug a little deeper. He asked me about my story—who I was, what my life was like. And though I was guarded, there was something about him that made me feel safe enough to open up, even if just a little.

As I shared bits and pieces of my life, I noticed how he listened. His eyes would light up when I talked about the good things, and his heart seemed to break when I spoke about my struggles. He didn't interrupt or offer advice right away. Instead, he listened—truly listened—as if my story was a gift he was receiving.

Eventually, I mentioned that I had to go to summer school because I'd failed the seventh grade. As soon as I said the words, I felt the walls I'd built up to protect myself from being known start to crumble. I hadn't told anyone about this secret, though I knew it was only a matter of time before everyone would know. That one sentence held so much weight—I felt embarrassed, exposed, and unsure of what to do next. I wanted to run and not look back, but the weight of whatever this feeling was paralyzed my ability to move.

I couldn't speak. There were literally zero words that could express the shame and guilt I felt. In my mind I replayed all the ways I could've and should've done things differently. This youth guy broke the silence with a question: "What do you feel like?" This was followed by a very long pause on my part. Again, he asked that same question but added two small words: "What do you feel like, right now?"

Without a doubt I was not comfortable. *What in the world did I just get myself into? Run, Michael, run!* All this was screaming inside my head.

"I feel like a failure," I said. And just like the feeling of a movie being paused right as an intense scene of chaos was about to occur, there we both were.

I attached this label of failure to how I saw myself and what I believed to be true about me.

Then he asked me a question that would change everything. "Do you know the difference between facts and truth?"

I had no idea what this guy was talking about.

He smiled and said, "It's a *fact* that you failed the seventh grade, but the *truth* is you are not a failure. Just because you make a mistake doesn't make you a mistake."

I had never heard anyone put it that way before. That simple conversation shifted something deep inside me. This guy was modeling values and self-worth concepts in a way I had not been exposed to. I had been defining myself by my mistakes, by the things I had gotten wrong. But for the first time, I realized that wasn't the whole picture. I wasn't a failure; I had simply made a mistake (though not a small one), and there was a difference.

That summer, I began to see myself in a new light. Things at home were still difficult—my mom's dysfunctional relationship with her husband, and the unhealthy way my mom and biological dad treated each other—but now, I had a different understanding. I realized that despite my environment, it was possible to change how I let it affect me. I also saw my parents in a different light. When the fighting and tension seemed unbearable, I would think, *Wow, I wonder what truths they believe about themselves that have caused this relationship to be the way it is.* For me, this breakthrough was huge.

It's amazing how one caring person can change the way we see ourselves and others. That youth minister didn't fix my problems, but he helped me break free from one of the negative beliefs I had about myself. He reminded me that we are all more than the sum of our mistakes.

As parents, we all want our children to reach their greatest potential. It can be so hard to watch them make mistakes, but those experiences are essential for their growth. The challenge for us is to guide them without smothering them, remembering that their mistakes are not a reflection of bad parenting but something better—a way of parenting that gives permission for us to learn with them when mistakes happen.

One student demonstrated quite eloquently their need for an opportunity to be allowed to make mistakes:

> I wanted to be encouraged in my dreams, even if they are ridiculous. I wish they'd encourage my dreams instead of break them, and have faith in what I do. I can see them judge me, but I wish they knew that I can take on responsibilities and make some decisions myself.

To let our children make mistakes, we have to give them the benefit of the doubt and a good dose of breathing room. This models trust and builds their self-confidence.

In this chapter, we explore how our children are shaped by the behavior modeled by the people closest to them. If you're curious about what is being modeled, start by asking questions and observing the five people they spend the most time with. What you'll discover is a path being formed—one that needs careful evaluation. We're not aiming for perfection but rather, we're building a mindset that recognizes how valuable lessons often come when we miss the mark and show us what we must do to make it better.

MESSY BEGINNINGS, MASTERFUL OUTCOMES

Years ago, I was invited to participate in a thirty-day silent retreat in Cleveland, Ohio. Thirty days! Me, the guy who can't stop talking, had to be quiet. When I first arrived, I struggled to communicate without using my voice. I found it challenging to find novel ways to express my personality, opinions, wants, and needs without talking.

A few days into the retreat, I was in line for the buffet next to a guy who I would later learn was a retired silent retreat guide master. Standing in line for lunch, minding my own business (silently, oh so silently), the retired guide crooked his neck toward me and whispered, "*Psst.* You wanna talk?" He said it like he was offering me a swig of bourbon in the middle of a Sunday church service. It was funny, of course, because he was just asking if I wanted to talk, but it was also fascinating. These retreat guides are no joke! They are highly trained to pick up on subtle, silent cues, and boy, did he have my number about my insatiable need to gab—without my having said a word.

Needless to say, I enthusiastically responded, "Um, yes, please," to his open invitation to chat.

The retired guide told me where I could find him during breaks, and so I made a habit of visiting his office every other day or so. One afternoon, he asked if I had ever thrown pottery. I hadn't. Admittedly, I also didn't know what "throwing pottery" really meant. Turns out that ceramics was a bit of a passion for this guy, and he offered to teach me more about it. We would be doing some literal modeling, but I had no idea that it would turn into more than that for me. Even as adults, we still seek figures who can guide and shape us in some beneficial way, and I was certainly open to learning something from this individual.

On clay day, we walked over to an outlying shed on the retreat grounds. It felt like a field trip from back when I was in school. All these amazing ceramics were inside, stacked shelf over shelf. Bowls, vases, pitchers, you name it. So beautiful. I didn't own much pottery, and I definitely had never made any myself, but I was intrigued. The retired retreat guide sensed my curiosity and asked if I'd like to try making a piece. I'm always up for something new, so of course I said, "Yeah! Let's do it!"

He handed me a lump of clay and told to me to throw it onto the electric pottery wheel. He said something about how my hands were the tools that would mold the clay into the desired form. I nodded along—uh-huh, yep, gotcha. I had no idea what he meant, but we were gonna try this anyway!

I clicked the wheel on and threw down the clay. You'd think I'd start small, show some reservation, but for better or for worse, I don't do anything small. I pushed the pedal all the way down and gave it some gas. The wheel started spinning and gray sludge splattered everywhere. I felt like a total fool trying to impose my will over this piece of clay. I felt frustrated. And then I got mad.

But this retreat master just laughed. He was doing what a parent might do with a child—patiently watching a child learn from their mistakes and having a great sense of humor about it!

I whined, "What are you laughing at? It's not funny! Look at this mess!"

"It's funny, because now we get to take your mess and learn from it. Let's talk about what didn't work, and then I'll show you how to mold the clay into something better. You wouldn't have been able to truly listen unless you had first experienced the beginnings of the process yourself."

The retired retreat master proceeded to show me how to properly throw the clay, starting with just a little bit of water on the pedal. Little by little, the clay was shaped into something I might actually use, even admire. This followed a process that made this art relatable. The clay must endure the temperature of the thousand-plus-degree heat in the kiln for its transformation to take place. Without this process, the clay would never mature into a durable ceramic.

After modeling the actions of my teacher, I ended up making a coffee mug. I couldn't believe that in a matter of an hour or two, I was able to do something I didn't think was possible, especially because my first attempt was such a failure.

SHOWING THE WAY

Our kids' messes can become powerful messages. We're all *molded* by someone or something, but to be molded correctly, we need to have the correct way of doing things *modeled for us*. We all know the expression "Actions speak louder than words." This is never truer than when we're communicating with children. Our kids watch our every move. They learn more lessons in the home through observation than they do through speech. We need to be intentional in our actions for modeling to work. Talk isn't enough for their environmental development. Our own behavior is the silent way they will learn most from.

As parents, we come with our own past experiences that arm us with the wisdom to see many steps ahead of our kids' actions. But remember, while we can already predict how a scenario will likely play out down the road, our children probably cannot. Our job is to understand where they are in that moment and model just the next step or two ahead. For the one being molded, it's impossible to grasp steps eight, nine, and ten if you haven't lived and learned the lessons required in steps five, six, and seven.

When I was young, there was no way I could really understand what it would mean in the long run if I cut class. What I *did* understand was the desire to avoid detention. One or two steps ahead was about as far as my reality would allow me to comprehend. Ending up without a high school diploma, or worse, in a miserable job, was just too far out there.

Sure, your fulfilling marriage, friendships, and career might set a good example and model for others—but you had to take a bunch of small steps on your own journey to finally arrive where you are today. And so do your kids.

How do we allow our kids to walk their own path while guiding them along the way? Communication and observation. Being a patient, helpful, and loving presence in their life without smothering them.

One satisfied child wrote in their letter:

> I am grateful for them driving me around and dealing with me when I was a rowdy kid. Thank you for searching for me when I ran off in the stores. Humoring me. Letting me sleep in. For always doing whatever you can to make me happy. They are great role models, and I love them.

Taking the time to do the things you know matter to your child models compassion and kindness—attributes that you want your kids to take into their adult lives for a whole variety of reasons. Sitting down with them once a week and encouraging them to talk about their ups and downs, wins and losses, is worth the time it will take for them to start sharing.

Now here's the twist: You, as the parent, share your wins and losses as well. Doing so consistently will create a bridge that will break down the generational divides. Once we build this regular rapport, your kids will find it easier to come to you with the big stuff, the hard stuff, and the uncomfortable stuff. Practicing observation and awareness of what is happening throughout our day is the goal—seeing ourselves and our kids at a deeper level. In this context, let's keep it simple and look at observation and awareness this way:

> Observation: What is happening around me?
> Awareness: What should my response be, if any?

This practice will help us be present as well as intentional, which could eliminate many decisions that place us in situations we never should have been in in the first place. We will see firsthand what others around us are modeling and level up our ability to discern faster if this is really what we would like to model—or in today's reality, to be known for.

Teaching our kids to do this by modeling it for them by our own actions will benefit them for years to come. Everything is a process, and modeling good behavior is no exception. All of us remain in process until the day we die. You are the greatest influence in your children's lives, and they need to know that you are not going anywhere and are not giving up on yourself or them. It's okay if they know you're still learning—wonderful, in fact—but you should also feel confident that you have a lot to teach and offer.

But here's the caveat: Modeling is a double-edged sword. We also have the power to model bad behavior if we're not careful. When we slip up (and we all slip up), we need to take ownership of our actions.

One student wrote, *Growing up, I felt I was never told how much my parents learned from their mistakes. I want to know what it was like for them.* If we slip up and model bad behavior, showing our children how we fix it, with an emphasis on the fact that nobody is perfect, can be a useful approach on multiple levels. It models realistic expectations and teaches our kids not to be their own worst critics.

Something I hear over and over from kids is that they feel they are held to a different standard of accountability than other people in their lives. This can include siblings, other family members, and close family friends. We have learned that many times our intention as parents is to help our kids by saying, "Why can't you be more like so and so?," but what your child can wind up feeling is more along the lines of "I guess I'm not good enough" or "I will never measure up." Spending time noticing what they *are* doing right is essential.

One student, in his letter, pleaded, *I wish my parents would understand the amount of work I put in to make them proud.* Another wrote, *I wish my parents knew that no matter how stubborn I get, I still listen to them and value everything that they say.*

Your kids really do hear *everything* you say. The reminder for us as parents is to accept the responsibility that our influence will always carry a weight very few will ever come close to—we are top-priority models for our kids. Our willingness to learn from the moments we fail and make it right will teach our kids how to do that for themselves, and one day maybe even for their own children.

FROM MODELING TO MULTIPLYING

All that said, models beyond our immediate family are important and necessary. Engaging our children with their community can be beneficial for both the community and our children's own growth. Every year, I speak to thousands of students with the hope of helping them see and believe the miracle and gift that they are to themselves, their families, and the world. I like to think of our events as immersive experiences to equip kids to make decisions their future selves will thank them for. We also develop curriculum and initiatives, and one particular project we adopted is called the Impact Project. This idea not only helps students see their own significance but also inspires them to use their gifts and abilities to help others.

When giving talks in schools, I set the stage by sharing examples of impactful projects other youth have done. Then I ask if anyone felt they were waiting for an opportunity to make a difference.

One day, three hands shot up, and I called them up to the front. I informed them, as I had previous groups, that participating in the Impact Project required a commitment to do three things:

1. Multiply the gift they were about to receive.
2. Find a person or cause in their own community that could use some help, and begin the process of "multiplying the gift" to benefit them.
3. Report back and share what they'd done.

The students agreed, and the "gift" I gave each of these three students was a fifty-dollar bill. I thought their eyeballs were going to pop out of their heads! I then reassured them that whatever they did, I was confident it was going to be impactful. I believed in them. Never in my wildest dreams could I have predicted how much good would come from this. One story in particular has always remained close to my heart.

These students began to ask around their community for ways they could help someone in need, and that's how they were introduced to a beautiful young boy named Lucien who had been diagnosed with leukemia. When these students heard about Lucien's story, they went all in. Each used their fifty dollars to buy materials to create wristbands that said "Stay Strong, Lucien." They sold them at sporting events, fairs, and other public gatherings with the intention of multiplying the original gift. When people heard about Lucien and these bracelets, they wanted to do anything they could to help make a difference for Lucien and his family.

In the end, these students raised close to twenty-five-hundred dollars! They did it all on their own. The school held a special assembly for Lucien's family and presented the check to them. As it turns out, twenty-five-hundred dollars was the amount his family needed to cover a month's worth of expenses, meaning Lucien's parents could spend more precious time with their son without having to worry about that month's financial burden.

Sadly, Lucien lost his battle with leukemia, but his life will remain a defining moment of hope, sacrifice, love, and generosity in the eyes of his community. I believe his life also inspired other youth to realize they had the power to get out there and make a difference. You are never too young (or too old) to create change for good.

This story still leaves me speechless. It reminds me that if we lay the right foundation, our kids will be able to do things we've only dreamed of. Our job isn't to do everything for them. Rather, it's to give them the opportunities to discover what they are capable of. The outcome may not always be as significant of a story as how the three students supported Lucien's family in their time of need. What's most important is that our kids should never be afraid to act, even if they think it requires more than they feel they can give. If we want to be good models for our children, we can start by showing them that they can in fact make an impact.

FINAL THOUGHTS

Like the retired retreat master showing me how to mold clay, it's our job as guides to not only talk to our children about how to behave in their community but also model the ideal (vision/mission) your family is striving for. Some days our lessons feel futile because our kids are messy, talk back, or are lazy, but don't give up! If your child does the right things out in the real world, it's a sign you're showing them what the good looks like, and that's a win!

As we pay attention and watch our kids grow up, we must be mindful of the labels they attach to themselves. They will express this through how they speak, how they dress, what they listen to, and with whom they spend their time. We must be careful not to try and over-control some of these areas, but without a doubt, they are a window into how our kids see themselves and the world around them.

Consider what it was like when you were a kid and the support, direction, and understanding you needed from your parents at the age your kid is now.

As much as possible, commit to modeling what the ideal looks like. This will mold our children at minimum to have a better sense of what is bad, good, better, and best in the situations they face. Nobody will get every day just right, but if we lead with the intention to model well, we'll all likely get it right more days than not.

ACCEPT

You were a child before you were a parent, and your child deserves the same opportunity.

REFLECT

What did you need from your parents when you were the age of your kid? As you take time to think about this, remember that being a kid today is not the same as it was for you. Patience is required.

There is a big difference between needs and wants that is difficult for kids to separate. Focus on the need. This will bring clarity and understanding as you provide the support they need today.

CONNECT

Practice patience by responding versus reacting.

Here are a few suggestions to help:

- Pause and reflect: What does my kid need from me right now?
- Think before you speak: Is what I'm about to say helpful and necessary?
- Be mindful of your tone. How you come across with your words is just as important as what you say.
- Take a minute. If you find yourself frustrated or overwhelmed, hold off while you take a moment to reset, and come back to the conversation with a clear head.

THINGS I WISH MY PARENTS KNEW . . .

I want to be strong and independent, but I do need help. I want to try new things, and I want you to believe in me. I'm not as brave as I seem. I need room to grow, but I also need you to be there when I fall.

—

I wish my parents knew how scared I am of failure; I want to be able to try, but I don't believe I can.

—

I wish you knew that at this point in my life, I'm afraid to tell anyone anything in fear of being judged.

—

I think of you every day when I'm not with you. It really helps when I feel scared.

SIX

Facing Fear

When was the last time you were really scared to try something new? Like terrified of what lay on the other side of that hurdle? Maybe you never thought of yourself as the type of person to have ever considered doing this *thing*, but there you were, considering it anyway. Curiosity had gotten the best of you. In a good way! Getting out of our comfort zone and challenging ourselves to try new things shouldn't stop when we have children, and it's important that we continue to model this kind of bravery. In this chapter, I discuss ways to avoid getting stuck in a rut by continuing to do the things we must do, even when they scare us.

I'll never forget the day curiosity tested me one August afternoon when I was about eleven years old. Texas is as hot as you think it is during the summer, and we often went to the nearby public swimming pool to cool off. It was a huge, Olympic-sized pool, and it had not one, not two, but *five* diving boards. My friend Jesse and I loved jumping off the boards, but we could only handle the small and medium-sized ones. The highest springboard looked okay, but we just hadn't worked up the nerve to climb it yet. Then there were the platforms—the kind that elite divers flip from. There were two of them, and they didn't bounce. The first level was high enough, but the second one . . . well, the second one may as well have been in outer space. Anytime somebody would jump off that thing, the whole pool would stop and watch. I thought the person doing it must be crazy, but it was amazing.

At some point that summer, Jesse and I started scheming that we should jump off the highest platform. Get all the notoriety. All the attention. This was just a pipe dream, of course. There was no way we had the guts to get up there.

Until one sweltering summer day, Jesse, totally deadpan, turned to me and said, "Michael, I think you can do it. Jump off the highest platform."

"Say what?"

"Come on. Just try it."

I was always the kid willing to try crazy stunts, and Jesse was smart enough to play right into that part of my personality. He knew that with just a little coaxing, there was no way I could say no to a challenge. So up I went—starting my ascent into the stratosphere. As I reached the halfway point of the first level, I thought, *Man, this is pretty high*. But I kept climbing. At the first level, my gut told me to stop. I looked down at Jesse and my other friends, and they were egging me on. The encouragement seemed to lift me higher and overpower any instinct that was trying to warn me to turn around. I climbed until I reached the very top of the highest platform.

The wind felt stronger up there, and I'm not that big of a guy. Never mind jumping, I was worried I might get blown away! I made the mistake of walking to the edge and looking down. Game. Over. There was no way that I was *ever* going to jump off that platform. So I inched back toward the ladder. Jesse and our friends were at the bottom, giving me a look like *What are you doing?*

I placed my foot on the top rung, ready to climb down, when the lifeguard lost his mind. He started blowing that whistle like crazy as if I couldn't hear him. Oh, I could hear him. I just chose not to pay attention. As the whistle blew louder and longer, all eyes shifted to the commotion between the lifeguard and me.

This teenage authority figure started shouting. He said I wasn't allowed to climb down. Apparently pool policy dictated that if you climb to the top, there's only one way to the bottom.

In retrospect, I'm sure if I really needed to climb down, I could have, but around this time my ego kicked into overdrive. I was terrified for sure, but there was no way I was going to let anyone see me back down now.

I stayed up on that platform, but my legs were like two pieces of steel stuck in a cement block. I just couldn't make my feet move. I started to imagine living way up high forever, where the air was thin and hard to breathe. I reasoned that someone could helicopter in McDonald's when I got hungry.

I was frozen with panic. I angrily yelled down at Jesse, "This is all your fault, man!" That's when he realized I needed his help, so he started chanting, "Go, Michael, go. Go, Michael, go." I felt kind of emboldened by that, and then he got a little louder. "Go, Michael, go!" Then everyone at the pool started chanting along with him. "Go, Michael, go!"

I counted to three. I don't know why we do that. Maybe three gives us just enough time to summon the courage to do something and not enough time to back down from it.

One . . . The cheers grew louder. *Two* . . . clapping and cheering and shouting my name. *Three* . . . I launched into the unknown. In mid-air, my only thought was that I had just jumped over the swimming pool and would land with a splat on the other side. It would have been impossible to jump over the pool, but I only believed it when my feet made contact with the cool, chlorine-filled basin. I was in! I lingered for a moment at the bottom of the pool and then resurfaced to the cheers of everyone there. And you know what? I wasn't mad at Jesse anymore. I was excited—and I wanted to do it again! I felt such an adrenaline rush that I urged Jesse to come up the next time.

Jesse quietly bowed out. Mumbled something about needing to get home, and he was out of there. What's interesting is that while Jesse never climbed to the top, a lot of other people did that day. It sometimes takes just one person to show the way.

TRUST THE PROCESS

Have you ever been in a situation where you just knew you had to take that first step, even though everything on the other side of that decision was completely unknown? The other side might be completely good or not so good, but staying where you were was not an option.

The remarkable role that Jesse played in encouraging me to jump was to show me what a person with real integrity looks like. He didn't leave when I wasn't "cool" and was afraid. Instead, he stood there and supported me until I didn't need him anymore. The takeaway, I believe, is that we need to build strong circles of support, because when things get hard or scary, we want the right people with us. You have the right and responsibility to make sure your tribe is a group of people who will bring out the best in you while also being honest and real with you.

We must teach our kids to trust the right people—people who will be there for them when it matters most. I am reminded of something that happened to me when I was eighteen years old. I never grew up with brothers and sisters, but I had become close with a couple who had just had their first kid. His name was Jai Michael, and he became like a little brother to me.

One evening, I had the chance to babysit him, and I'll be honest, I was a little nervous. He was at the age when he was just learning to walk, and my level of stress trying to make sure he did not hurt himself was through the roof. We were in the living room when he looked at me and said, "Mikey, I want to hold you."

At first, I thought to myself, *That's impossible.* So I looked at him and said, "You can't hold me; I'm too big, and you are too small."

He looked at me again and repeated his intention: "Mikey, *I want to hold you.*"

Again, I thought to myself, *What is this kid thinking? There ain't no way.* And that's when Jai Michael took off running toward me. When he was about ten feet away, he launched himself into the air straight at me. I had a decision to make. I could catch him, or I could move out of the way and teach him not to fly at other human beings. Of course, I caught him and began to spin him in circles. Before I could set him down, he wrapped his little arms around my neck, placed his head on my shoulder, and said, "Mikey, I'm holding you."

He trusted that the one he was jumping to would catch him. And he was right. He also taught me that to accomplish what he knew he could do, he had to take a leap of faith. He knew he wasn't strong enough to pick me up and carry me around like I thought he was going to try and do. Instead, he accomplished his goal—and the only way I could understand what he meant was for him to show me.

FEARLESS STEPS FORWARD

When we're trying something new and bumping up against legitimate challenges or our own fear, we need to understand what our options are. Fear can be detrimental, but it can also become fuel to overcome just about anything. Eliminating fear requires massive action. Here are three ways to consider what fear can look like:

1. FEAR—false evidence appearing real. This type of fear requires us to evaluate the situation and gather as much information as possible. We must be honest with ourselves about what we think we know versus the truth of what it actually is. This will reveal what we must do next, even if the decision is hard.
2. FEAR—false expectations appearing real. This feeling can be overwhelming and crippling, to say the least. Whether

from the perspective of a parent or child, making known the expectations of a desired outcome is critical. We must be careful not to assume everyone understands our intentions or direction. When these expectations are unspoken or unclear, they tend to lead to confusion, disappointment, and frustration.

3. FEAR—face everything and rise. This approach takes courage. It's the decision to make a way, even when the path seems difficult and most likely uncertain. This might look like trying out for a team, talking to someone you feel a connection with, or moving on from a relationship that is not good for you.

We all need people in our lives who will help us see what we are capable of and encourage us to take the necessary action to live up to our potential.

One teenager searching for that kind of encouragement wrote, *I wish my parents knew that I love to play hockey but I'm nervous to ever ask my dad to bring me to tryouts; I don't like to try out because I don't want to get rejected.* When kids are scared of trying something new, they need the kind of people who will stand at the bottom of the high-dive platform and cheer them on. If you or your child is having a hard time finding the right people who will be on their side, you could start by being that kind of person for them.

Just like every golfer values their caddy's advice, your kids need your insight—but every golfer ultimately makes the final call, and we also need to let our kids own the decisions they commit to. If your kid has decided to try a new sport or group, we must show our support and teach them the value and importance of their role on that team.

We all know that things don't always go as planned. Sometimes, we feel comfortable and are confident we've found our place. Other times, we find ourselves in situations where we're scared or nervous, even asking for help through a prayer to get through it. We learn that the better we prepare, the better chance we have to achieve what we set out to do. But what happens when things don't go the way we hoped, prayed, or planned for? The frustration, disappointment, and feeling of "how did I miss this?" can really mess with our confidence.

MAPPING OUR PATH

Let's look at it like a map. Today's maps are super advanced—they show us how to get from point A to point B, warn us about accidents, traffic, and even speed traps. Sometimes, they even reroute us when we don't know what's ahead. Our job is to trust the map, even when advised to take a different road. But if you're like me, you've probably ignored the rerouting directions before, thinking you knew better. And while it sometimes works out, most of the time I've ended up stuck in traffic, frustrated, and wondering why I didn't just listen in the first place.

A map shows us where we are, where we're going, and the best way to get there—eliminating the "fear of the unknown." Now, imagine using an old-school map—you know, the kind that's folded a bunch of times and impossible to open up all the way. Once you finally find where you are on the map, you get a little excited because you're one step closer to your destination. But then, you have to figure out how you want to get there. Do you take the fastest route, such as a highway with tolls, or do you decide to make a couple of stops along the way? Maybe there's a cool place you want to visit or a restaurant you've always wanted to try. Whether you take the direct route or choose to make stops, both are valid choices.

But here's the important part: Why are you choosing the path you're on? Do you want to get there quickly because you're on a deadline or because you just want it to be over with? Are you delaying because you're avoiding something? The map shows us our current reality. Without it, we might find good things to do along the way, only to realize we made it to our destination too late.

Today's world often tells us to do whatever feels right, and to be honest, that sounds really intriguing. But if thirteen-year-old me always did what felt right, I don't know if I'd be here today, living this amazing life.

Our job as parents is to help create the map for our kids, allowing them to be comfortable making difficult and, at times, scary decisions. It's okay to accept that things will be hard. The best things in life often require sacrifices that are difficult and scary. Self-control is hard. Doing the right thing is hard, so help your children through these "stopping points" on their map, reminding them of their destination, where they want to be, and how best to get there. Remember to ask questions so you have an understanding of how they see their map and what the scariest stops are for them. When roadblocks pop up, the map helps remind us of where they are and where they need to go and that detours are okay and may even help keep them safe.

I want to share something I've learned from the letters we've received. When we rely on our feelings alone to decide what's right or true in a scary situation, things can get confusing. What seemed true, or safe, at thirteen might not at sixteen. Many influences can add to the confusion and bewilderment of growing up. *I wish my parents understood that peer pressure is different today than it was years ago,* one student wrote, *and some days we can't avoid it.* For a child or teen, entering a new classroom or attending an after-school event or party can be like standing on the high-dive platform.

In many of my talks, I share the idea that we can either be a thermostat or a thermometer. A thermometer tells us the temperature, but a thermostat changes it. Think of it like walking into a room where everyone seems to be in a bad mood—that can be a scary prospect for a young person. That part is like being a thermometer, just reading the mood around you, which is an important first step in turning apprehension into curiosity. But then, being a thermostat—that can change the mood of the space. You have the power to walk into that same room and change the atmosphere by your attitude. Maybe you can't always avoid the situation—like going to school or work or a social event you had no desire to attend—but you can choose how you respond, whether you are scared of the space or willing to shape it with your presence. You don't have to let the environment control you. A conversation with our children about this can help give them the confidence they need when faced with scenarios they are reluctant to participate in, or even dreading.

Sometimes, when I'm speaking to a group, I see smiling faces, and everyone looks engaged. But my attention is often drawn to the one or two people who look like they'd rather be anywhere else. It's uncomfortable, a little like being frozen in place on the diving platform ladder. I start wondering, *What can I do to lift their spirits?* But you know what? Most of the time, those very people are the ones who come up to me afterward and share how much my talk meant to them. It's a reminder that we don't always know what's going on in other people's minds. Hyper-focusing on that unknown can enhance our fear.

So, when we're scared or uncertain, it's okay to keep moving forward. Trust the map, what you want to achieve. It might not always show you the whole journey, but it helps you remember where you are and where you're going. And that's enough valid information to help you confidently take the next step forward.

FINAL THOUGHTS

If you're stuck in a rut or feel like you're not making your greatest contribution as a parent at this time, think about the things that make your heart beat fast and your fears scream loud. Find the courage and do the thing you hope your child would be willing to do when facing uncharted territory. Let us not live a life of regret about what could have been or, worse, what *should* have been. Not only will your future self thank you for this, but these are the kind of decisions that your kids will never forget and will forever be grateful for.

ACCEPT

We will get stuck in our fear from time to time, as will our kids. Encouragement has the power to unlock the courage your child needs to overcome whatever obstacle they are facing.

REFLECT

Courage is the virtue that reveals what we are capable of doing, even when we feel scared. The power of this virtue is unlocked the second we are honest about why we would consider not being courageous. Asking for help is an act of courage that will silence our fears and shine a light on where our focus needs to be. What is one area in your personal life and role as a parent you could ask for help with?

CONNECT

Acknowledge and reward the courageous moments, and you will see them repeated on a level that will change the world for the better.

Here are some suggestions to help:

- When your kids are scared, unsure, or concerned, don't rush to fix the problem; instead, help them define what's holding them back. Help them define their map.
- Talk with them about the potential outcomes of being courageous in this situation and, when they are ready, suggest how to take the first step (showing up is usually step one).
- Work to always keep things in the light, nothing hidden. You are their parent, and if you are not involved, your kid will search and eventually find someone or something to fill the void you left behind.
- Any attempt to act courageously merits your acknowledgment and praise—this validation is the fuel your kids need to develop this virtue.

THINGS I WISH MY PARENTS KNEW . . .

I wish my dad would get more involved in my life.

–

I wish my parents remembered my birthday.

–

I wish my parents knew how much I have fun with them.

SEVEN

Do You See Me?

Being present and available for our children is one of our most important responsibilities as parents. Our children need to know we see them, we love them, and we'll be there for them no matter what. In this chapter, I discuss ways to prioritize our time and resources to ensure we're being present for the most important people that have been entrusted to us. I'm certain that most of us, myself included, could do even better there.

I certainly remember a few of those moments, and one of them sticks out.

I had just returned home from an intense week on the road. As I approached the front door, I was incredibly excited to see my family. There's always an excitement in the room when I get back—lots of hugs and kisses and jumping up and down. If you've had little kids, you've probably experienced some of that magic yourself.

I learned a valuable lesson that day about not taking these precious moments for granted. My daughter, Hannah, who was quite young at the time, was taking dance lessons and was wearing one of her ballet outfits that evening. She ran up when I walked in the door, gave me a squeeze, and said, "Daddy, I missed you." It was one of those special parenting memories any one of us would carry through the rest of our lives—except for the fact that I nearly missed what was right in front of me.

My wife, always the observer and listener, was watching this all go down from the kitchen. I hugged Hannah and then walked right past her to sit down and open my laptop. There's always a bunch of people that require immediate responses after I've held a week's worth of live events, many of whom share powerful feedback, so I try not to let too much time pass before I respond.

Just as I cracked open the computer, Hannah planted herself squarely in front of me and said, "Dad, watch me dance."

I wanted to watch *in theory*, but I was busy doing "important" work, and so I told Hannah to wait a minute. I just wanted to get through some of my emails and then she could have my full attention. But that little voice got louder. "Dad, watch me dance."

I said, "Hannah, please wait. Just let me finish my work." She wasn't going to wait. She came up close, raised her tiny hand, and slammed my laptop shut. Just like that.

Whoa. My girl meant business. There was nothing I could do. All I saw were these beautiful green eyes blinking at me, simply asking me to take a moment to watch what she had learned in class.

For what amounted to thirty seconds, Hannah swirled around five or six times and did a few leaps through the air before she got distracted, as little kids do, and took off running toward the next shiny thing. Thirty seconds! That's all she needed to feel like she was the most important person in my life. How did I almost miss that or mess up something that's so obvious to see now? Why did I feel that those people on the other end of my inbox required my immediate attention when there was my own daughter, right in front of me, telling me plainly that she needed me?

After that short and perfect performance, I was all alone again. Just my laptop and me, ready to handle whatever emails or files or social posts needed tending to. I glanced over at my wife, who had this smile on her face, and I knew what it meant. She was reminding me that all that "important" work I do could never hold a candle to everything going on within my very own home.

I simply had to be willing to pause what I was doing to be present for the most important people in my life.

THE GIFT OF PRESENCE

On one occasion, after one of my speaking events, a young man walked up to me and introduced himself as Jack. He looked to be about twenty years old. I'd just shared a story about losing someone very close to me. With his hands in his pockets, Jack said, "You know, my grandpa meant so much to me. But he passed away, and I never got to say what I wanted to say to him."

"What did you want to say to him?" I asked.

"I just wanted to tell him how much I loved him," Jack said.

"Don't you think he knows that?"

Jack shrugged and nodded.

"Close your eyes and think of all the good things about your grandfather that you remember," I gently told him.

As this young man closed his eyes, I could see they were welling up with tears. He smiled when I asked what he was thinking about.

"My grandfather always made me feel special. When we were

together, I was the most important person in the room. He asked me what I thought about stuff, like he really cared about my opinion, and I always felt like he was happier when I was around."

Wow. That hit home for me. This man's grandfather was wise enough to remember what was required in the moment and what needed to wait until after his grandkids were off doing something else. And look at the impression it left on his grandson! I was grateful to Jack for telling me his story. It reminded me that our undivided attention is another great gift we can give and that the recipient can feel how special that gift really is.

I sometimes struggle with prioritizing the people who need my attention the most, because my entire job revolves around being there for others. It's so easy to get bogged down with the daily busyness of things, and to tell ourselves we're doing all this to provide for our families, or because we have no choice, that it's our job. How many of us have even become defensive about our decisions when confronted by our loved ones and found ourselves saying things like "What do you want me to do, just quit my job?"

We all have to work, and I'm not suggesting that anyone quit their job as a quick-fix solution to this problem. But ask yourself, has the amount of time you spend at work versus the time you spend with your family created tension? Has your family repeatedly asked you, even begged you, to come back to them and leave work behind occasionally? What slight adjustments can you make to bridge this gap?

Thinking back on that evening with Hannah, I could have been smarter from the get-go. If I knew (which I did) I had to respond to some emails, I should have stopped at a coffee shop to tick those items off my list before getting home. Sure, I would have come home a bit later, but I would have saved my kids from having to experience the disconnect between seeing the physical me while the mental, emotional, and spiritual me hadn't caught up yet.

If I have learned anything from these letters, it's that our kids are dying to spend time with us. *I wish my parents knew what makes me happy. It's not the gifts*, one child wrote. We can fill in the blanks here—quality time. Kids want their parents to know that they love hanging out with them, even when their words and actions might make their parents think otherwise.

You are the consistent light in your child's life, the one person they need and want to count on. No matter what happens, they desire to believe and know you are on their side.

It's time we begin to make the time, because we won't have a lot of it once our kids grow up, move out, and get involved in their own lives and families. Acknowledge that nobody can do everything, but you can always do something, even on your bad days. If 50 percent is all you've got in a given moment, that's okay—you gave 100 percent of what you felt you had. You gave the best you possibly could that day to make time to be there for the people who matter the most to you.

When we feel we've got to do everything and be there for everyone, what often ends up happening is that we make time for everyone except for our own families. If being there for your kid means you need to physically write down "spend time with family" in the calendar, do it! We don't want to wind up being the parent whose child is so forlorn that she writes a letter about it: *My life is harder than it seems. I wish my parents paid attention to me. I exist. . . . I'm still here.*

I wish that they would give attention to me like before. Or the parents of the child who is begging to be noticed: *I want you to ask about my life. I want you to talk to me. I don't care what it's about; I just want you to stop thinking about work and money and just take the time to talk to your child.*

If we don't do the important work at home, and there's a disconnect between your words and actions, bitterness can settle in within your kids. We all have a fundamental desire to be seen and heard. It's how we fill up our emotional tanks. But if we're not paying attention, our kids might go looking for other ways to fill their tanks—seeking out people and places that prey on and take advantage of youth who are craving that desire to be seen and heard.

We've been given today. That's 24 hours, 1,440 minutes, 86,400 seconds. The greatest gift you can give is your time. Make sure you're giving it to the right people.

TOO FAST, TOO SOON

Every year, I get my eyes checked. To this day, I always get a little bit nervous about that appointment. I never did very well on tests in school, and the annual eye exam makes me sweat. You know how it goes—the doctor puts a contraption in front of your eyes, clicks a bunch of lenses, and asks if you see better or worse, better, or worse. It's not always easy to decide, and I don't know why I always feel like I'm not answering the question correctly. But eventually, as the optometrist fine-tunes the instruments, everything finally snaps into place, and I can now see more clearly. This change was made with tiny adjustments.

Our vision gets foggy when we stop paying attention and coast along using the old prescription. I cannot always rely on yesterday's success to carry me through today's challenges. Of course, the wisdom obtained from experience is invaluable, but we still must be willing to make slight adjustments along the way.

As our kids grow up, they are not the same children they once were. This can be hard for any parent to accept. When they were young, it felt like we would have a lifetime together, and before you know it, they're entering junior high, high school, and university. If we take the time to truly see them, then perhaps all of this can fly by a little more intentionally, and we can miss out on less.

In regard to kids growing up fast, not taking the time to see our kids can have other consequences as well. Over the course of many years working with youth, I have seen that the things people used to do and experience once they got to college more often than not now happen in high school. The things that used to be typical high school behavior are now happening in junior high, and the things that were done in junior high are now happening in elementary school. With everything from physical relationships to the way kids talk to one another, certain milestones you would expect from particular age groups are dropping to younger brackets faster than we realize. The innocence of our kids is being taken away at a younger age than ever before, and it's only speeding up. I don't mean to scare you; I just want to shine a light on a reality that may help you. Clear vision helps us see better, but you have to actually see your kids in the first place to see them clearly.

Recently, I was asked to speak at an elementary school. I don't typically speak for elementary schools, but I have been receiving more inquiries in the last few years than ever before. Prior to this event, I asked the principal, "So why have you called and asked me to come to your school? You know I typically talk to junior high and senior high students, right?"

The principal replied, "Well, the things the kids are going through in elementary are not what we're expecting or used to seeing."

I said, "What are you talking about? I would expect bullying, but is it more than that?"

She replied, "Yeah, we have some kids who are on suicide watch in grade four."

"Grade four!" My heart sank.

Why are kids' experiences skewing younger and younger? I think one major reason has got to be their exposure, or overexposure, to information. Children are naturally curious, and it's apparent that technology has given them access to topics they're not yet prepared to navigate.

It's a big responsibility to help them navigate those topics, but they will appreciate your efforts. Kids generally do want help, even if they don't always show it.

I wish you were there to help me through everything, one student wrote in her parent letter. *I want your help.* In this age of information overload, there is an especially urgent need to be there for young and vulnerable minds.

And when are they most susceptible to the information their technology throws at them? Kids usually become deeply aware about what their peers think of them around grade three. That's about the time a child will start to think, *Oh, man, am I dressed the right way? Do I have the cool backpack?* Stuff like that. And now it's been turned up a notch, because now they have to worry if they have the latest device, enough followers, and so much more. This idea of comparison has been amplified and then introduced at younger and younger ages. Then throw in the online alternate reality of beauty standards, wealth, and just having so much stuff. More and more stuff.

This is when our kids really need to be seen by us, to make sure this alternate reality doesn't alter or compromise their present reality.

Yes, the information age has brought us really great things, too. For example, you can develop an interest or craft so much faster than any generation before thanks to online tutorials and access to the world's best teachers on demand. But a lot of what we see is not based on reality. There's a whole other digital universe out there that is impossible to replicate in analog. And perhaps, as a result of them being able to learn everything online, and being so busy online ourselves, we are no longer developing our child's interests and doing things with them like we used to—again taking away from being present and seeing them. One student wrote, *I wish my parents knew that I want them to come to my soccer games.* Another wrote, quite perceptively, *I want you to see things that make me happy. They might seem weird, but I want you to notice them.*

It's not just that they want you to see them—they want you to see what they see, what they enjoy.

The broader point I want to share is that we just don't know exactly what it's like to be our kids' age because the world is so different now. Their normal is not what our normal was. Try to be patient and understanding and parent from a place of guiding and learning rather than using the phrase "Well, back in my day . . . ." This is a guaranteed eye-roll, and they are not necessarily wrong to feel this way. It's a whole new game out there now. The letters these kids have shared with us show us that they want us, as parents, to help them understand this world of connection. When we teach our kids the art of communicating face-to-face, we are preparing them to be equipped to communicate better in all other platforms—where they will be *seen* by many others.

FINAL THOUGHTS

As you guide your child into their next stage in life, the advantage you have is all you have personally experienced and overcome. There will be moments that you are unclear about what to do or how to help, and that is 100 percent normal. Trying to pretend that you know best or understand their situation when you don't is a guaranteed setback. Including them in your process of understanding and welcoming their help and insight will provide you a better and more effective direction to lead them as well as show them that you want to spend quality time with them to build toward something better. Together you will always be better, and sometimes their insight is the answer you need to move forward.

ACCEPT

Your child desires to be seen. And they desire to be seen not only through your perception but also through their reality.

REFLECT

You can see in your child what they may not yet see in themselves—you can guide them from the specific place in development and age they are with a flexible future self in mind for them. We cannot expect our kids to always get it right the way we want it. It has taken us this many years to find our rhythm, and there are probably a few things (multiplied) that we could do better. The goal is to amplify the good and help them see it in themselves.

CONNECT

We're never too old to play. Do something with your child or teen that would show them you notice what's important to them. Here are some suggestions to help:

- Whatever their favorite game is, attempt to play it with them.
- Create a playlist of their favorite songs, learn the lyrics, and shock them with your current swagger of vocal excellence and "good taste" in music.
- Plan a night out that is all about them (you may have to do some homework by asking their friends for suggestions).
- Cook their favorite meal with them.
- Write them a letter about a memory of when they were younger and how much that meant to you.

THINGS I WISH MY PARENTS KNEW . . .

I just wish my parents could maybe help me out a little more.

—

I wish I could tell them that I just want their approval.

—

I wish that I could be more loved.

EIGHT

Am I Enough?

What is truth? Webster defines it as the body of real things, events, or facts. This question is particularly more relevant in recent years, as the definition of truth has shifted from an objective reality to something more subjective, often influenced by feeling or emotion. The question of "Am I enough?" can certainly become a messy and subjective truth as well.

When I failed the seventh grade, what I believed at that time—my truth—was that I was a failure. While the statement "I failed" is a fact, the deeper truth was accepting that failure does not have to define me. I can fail a grade but still be enough by learning from the setbacks to set up a better and wiser version of me.

I love to pose this question at my events with teenagers: What happens when your truth, and their truth, and my truth collide? Which one is the ultimate truth?

This is usually when heads begin to tilt, which ignites the beauty and power of the mind. I then share what I consider to be one of the most powerful forces in their world: a mind made up. This idea often makes eyebrows squeeze together and question, "How in the world is a mind made up one of the most powerful forces?"

Consider the moments you decided to pursue something that you were advised not to do or possibly couldn't afford—physically, relationally, mentally, or financially; the second your mind was made up, you found a way and made it happen. You have proven to yourself how powerful you are when your mind is made up. Yet the reason I believe this is the most powerful force is because we have the *ability and permission* to change our mind.

STEPPING INTO THE LIGHT

I was giving a talk to a group of eleventh-grade students. During one of the breaks, a young man came up to me, looking focused and intense. I could tell he needed to talk, and I let him guide me toward a quieter space where he could speak freely.

This young man started out by saying, "What you said—it bothered me."

"Bothered you? Why did it bother you?"

"Because it made me think about something in my life that I know I have to change."

He proceeded to tell me that his family life hadn't been the greatest. His mom kicked him out of the house, and he had been living on his own for over a year. When I asked why his mom would do such a thing, he said it was because he hadn't been following the rules. I pried further.

"Tell me more about why she asked you to leave the house."

"Because I was doing things. I'm still doing things. Drugs. And my behaviors were starting to affect the family."

The drugs this kid was addicted to were intense. I just couldn't believe he was only in eleventh grade, but let that be a wake-up call to all of us parents who think our kids are too young to be exposed to things that have the power to hurt them and those closest to them. Time to get real!

He went on to divulge that he felt he had nothing left. That he had hit his rock bottom. He lost his family, his friends, everything.

I pointed out, "But you're still in school!"

He acknowledged that fact and said that school was all he had left. That the reason he showed up every day was that it was the only constant in his life and the only thing holding him together. Finally, he said he was ready to get help.

That was a huge moment: admitting there was a problem and asking for help.

I immediately called in a teacher who knew this student well and would be able to guide him toward the right support. But before going down that road, this teacher and I allowed ourselves to pause and listen quietly as the young man poured his heart out. He wasn't sure if he was strong enough to overcome his addictions, rebuild his relationship with his mom, and live a life he could be proud of. He was simply trying to cope as best he could with daily life, and the questions underlying his entire story revolved around whether he was *enough*.

What struggles do we need to bring into the light to believe and know we are enough? We cannot defeat what we cannot define. What remains hidden will never have the ability to see the light of truth. Buried pain can overwhelm us until we begin to implode from the inside out. It can make us feel small and powerless and like we are not enough. One of our jobs as parents is to draw out the darker parts within our kids and within ourselves to flood light into the parts we'd rather hide. We need to show our kids that even though we are complicated beings with both light and dark within, we are still worthy of love, respect, and attention. Our kids need to know that they are most definitely more than enough.

I often ask the following question when I'm speaking to large groups of students: "If I were to turn out all the lights, cover all the windows, and then turn on the world's smallest flashlight, would you be able to see it?" Typically, there are a few eye rolls, but eventually they respond yes.

"Would it be bright, or would it be dim?" I ask.

"Dim!" they shout back.

Then I ask, "The more you focused on it, would the light become dimmer or brighter?" The point I try to make is that what we focus on is what we can follow. The things we care about become brighter. I also point out that even if we sometimes feel that our light is insignificant, when we put all our lights together, the whole room can be dispelled of darkness.

Part of being enough is a *sense of belonging*—of belonging to that room full of lights, and being one of them, working together for some bigger purpose, or simply to comfort another. To be seen by the other lights.

That was what was missing for that young man.

BREAKING THROUGH THE DARKNESS

I am reminded of a story I learned about a father who asked his little girl what she would like for her birthday. He made it clear that there were no conditions on what she could ask for and told her to take some time to think about it. After a few minutes, she came running back to her dad and, without hesitation, said she wanted a flashlight. Though her dad was a bit confused, he had been a parent long enough to know that not only was this request easy enough to grant, but the cost would also be minimal—it was a win-win. The girl's birthday came, and when it was time to open the presents, he handed her the gift. Her eyes lit up with joy when she opened the gift, because it was exactly what she had asked for. Her dad couldn't take it anymore. He was confused about why she was so excited about a flashlight when she could have asked for something much bigger and undoubtedly more expensive.

"So, sweetheart, why did you want this flashlight?" he asked.

She took him by the hand and led him down a dark hallway in their home, leading him to a room she rarely walked to alone. She became a little tense the closer they got to the end of the hall, but with the flashlight and the grip of her father's hand, she kept going. Her dad knew she was scared of the dark, and when she turned on the flashlight, he asked where they were going. She said, "We're going to look for some darkness—I don't have to be afraid anymore, because I have the light!"

What this means for us is that we can recognize that our life, personality, abilities, and experience can become the light we have that leads us through our next step. In previous chapters, I discuss the importance of being seen. I also discussed overcoming fear. The darkness can cloud the truth, but we don't have to be scared to shine a light in those places. When someone, especially a parent, helps us to see—offers us a light—we ourselves are seen.

When a child is well-supported, they feel braver, safer, and more comfortable in their own skin. They become comfortable asking for the flashlight and will trust that their parents will help them when they feel overwhelmed or stuck. The father *saw* and *heard* his daughter when he fulfilled her unorthodox gift request—he helped her believe and know she was capable and enough to walk through the darkness.

Every parent can be the one who gives their child the flashlight, the tools they need to overcome obstacles and be enough. It may take work, but no one said being a parent was going to be an easy road. The day you found out that you were going to be a parent, you may have had mixed emotions. From then on, your life was no longer just about you. You were given the responsibility of loving and molding another life. This responsibility is a life-changing gift, and as parents we know it's not something that could be taken lightly. In the beginning, your child was formed in darkness. That darkness was a safe place to develop and grow. And though the darkness was safe for the moment, a light had to pierce it before you could hold that gift.

Darkness and light are two sides of the same coin. One needs the other. One is not inherently good or bad. They are both necessary, but the practice is in providing our kids with the right tools to have control and agency over the light and the darkness, and not the other way around.

RESTORATION AND GROWTH

Your children's fears and problems can hinder them from feeling like they are enough, just as they did for the young man who approached me, to a devastating extent. But the right words, spoken at the right time, have the power to help kids feel like they are enough and have what it takes. The narrative and context of showing them a renewed vision of how they see themselves will bring to light a gift we could all benefit from.

I like to use personal stories to enrich the talks I give to students along with using everyday examples that underscore a central theme or point I'm trying to make. For example, I often ask a group if they have ever jumped on a beach ball in the middle of a swimming pool. Most hands inevitably shoot up. Then I ask how many can hold their balance while submerging the beach ball underwater. I'm confident nobody can stay still for long. Finally, I ask what happens when you lose your center of gravity and fall off the ball. Does it stay under the water? No, of course it doesn't. The ball shoots up above the surface.

The students begin to understand that while we can submerge our problems in the short-term, we can't do it forever. All the pressure required to hold things down creates an even stronger opposing force that eventually brings everything to the surface.

We're all familiar with the phrase *The grass is greener on the other side*. But the truth is that the grass is greener where we choose to water and maintain the grass. And when we try to run away from problems or pretend that whatever needs to be dealt with isn't a big deal, the problem will follow us around until we finally confront it.

My hope is that you look at your kids through the lens of what could be. This is possible because of the fact that though some of the shattered and scarred parts of our own life story may never be restored to their original form, we have made it through and have become wiser because of them. This also proves to us that we are able to create a better and more beautiful tomorrow because of what we have learned, and that we are willing to heal through from pain of our own past. The goal is that tomorrow we become better than we were today. Though we are always *enough*, I also know I don't want to just get back to how I was a year ago; I want to become a better version of myself, and I believe you do as well.

Sometimes it's difficult for our kids to see what better looks like when they are trying to ignore or push down the problem right in front of them. Our job as parents is to help guide our kids, one step at a time, through the challenges they face and lead them into the light, so they will see the ability we already see in them.

What would you do if you learned something about your child that completely took you by surprise? And what if you discovered this through another couple, or a friend of your child's, leaving you confronted with the unsettling feeling that you don't truly know your child? Regardless of whether the information they shared with you was true, do you think your reaction would be more defensive or genuinely receptive?

I ask this because I've witnessed how parents sometimes dismiss important confrontations that need to be addressed because of their unwillingness to accept that their child has been called out. Speaking from personal experience as a father, such moments can create a full stop on everything else that had my attention.

Our kids' actions are not always a reflection of our parenting, but they can be clues to what our children feel they are missing. When there is something lacking in the relationship between parent and child, the child often seeks to fill that void in ways they know how, which can be hard for parents to accept.

That unsettled feeling we experience might reveal our lack of attention or provision, which led our child to seek something outside of the family bond. What I'm referring to here are the foundational elements every parent-child relationship must provide without question or judgment: to be loved, seen, heard, and safe. When any one of these needs is unmet, children will feel the absence and look to fill it elsewhere.

The challenge arises when kids try to meet these needs in ways that cross boundaries or go against family values. As parents, when we receive information that could lead to difficult conversations, it's essential to approach the situation with a mindset of restoration. We need to ask, "What can we do to restore this relationship and make it better than before?"

This might look like responding calmly when a child talks back, even though it creates a fracture in the relationship. While the offense might seem minor, the fracture is still real. Small fractures over time will create long-term pain and eventual separation if unattended to. Parenting with a restorative mindset allows us—and our kids—to understand that discipline is not about punishment or about the parent needing to prove a point; it's about restoring what is most important in our family connection.

Over time, as we embrace this approach, our children will come to appreciate the value of restoration. These moments of healing will become defining points as they grow and build relationships in their future.

FINAL THOUGHTS

Never diminish what someone else is going through, especially your child. It doesn't have to be as serious as addiction or abuse for the issue to matter deeply to them. Something as seemingly simple as not doing well on a test or not getting the coveted role in the school play can be tough! Maybe a friendship unraveled, or a romantic relationship just broke down. We've all been there. These are universal themes every person confronts. Can you step back and remember who was there for you when you were growing up? What would they say now? And if you didn't have a lot of support back then, change the story now! Be there for your child, as the person you needed when you were a kid.

When our kids wonder if they are enough, our answer, of course, is a resounding yes! Your child will always be more than enough. And you know what? You will always be more than enough, too. You are the one who will have the most powerful voice for them because you are the greatest influence in your child's life.

ACCEPT

The decisions we make today will determine the life we live tomorrow.

REFLECT

What are the top three values your family is known for? We all know too well that people can be paradoxical. What we have learned is that our kids want the same good things that we are known for in the public sphere to be bestowed on them in the home sphere. If you are a rockstar for your fellow employees, your friends, your church community, or even your extended family, but you're not the same person at home, there's a contradiction there that you will want to examine. Take some time to reflect on the version of you that you want your kids to tell their children about.

CONNECT

Create visual reminders of your family journey. Here are some suggestions to help:

- Create a family vision statement together and frame it on the wall.
- Take a family photo at least once a year.
- Start a daily gratitude journal that everyone contributes something to.
- Create a monthly video together.
- Get a map and place a pin where everyone in your extended family is from or lives.

THINGS I WISH MY PARENTS KNEW . . .

I hope they know that even if I don't always say it, I love them.

–

I am strong enough to do it, even if I feel weak at times.

–

I wish I could spend more time with them.

NINE

Prioritizing Hope

I believe two of our greatest gifts in life are time and people. And the two go hand in hand—we will always make time for the people who hold the highest importance in our lives.

The account balance of today is 24 hours, 1,440 minutes, 86,400 seconds. Each second that passes can never be repeated. There are countless stories of people who have been asked at the end of their lives what they would do differently if they could do it all over again. Without fail, most people respond that they would have spent more time with loved ones. This insight can help us refocus on the things that matter most. Let's look at today as a starting point. There are probably many things we would change if we could do it all over again, but as we already know, the gift of time will not allow us any repeat moments.

The gift of time also presents us with opportunities for growth. We can learn from the days that have passed to help us limit our mistakes in the future. And the only way this is possible is if we are willing to be honest about where we have been and where we are today.

As our kids get older, we are reminded that our time with them is getting shorter. And though we will always have influence in our children's lives, it is mission critical that the time we spend together now creates the memories and lessons that will guide them to a better tomorrow. Show your kid just how big a priority they are to you.

Each of us has more than enough time to live a life we are proud of with the people who make our life richer and more meaningful. But I have seen over the course of my career that the closer we get to people, the more we realize we need to work on ourselves. Nobody is asking for perfection, and even though we may demand more from others than we are willing to demand of ourselves, consider putting down the microscope and picking up the mirror. Do you see a reflection of truth, goodness, and beauty? If you do, you are actually generating hope in them—hope for a bright future.

INSPIRING HOPE

How important is hope for our kids? It is the answer to most of the problems they face. Recently, I heard an acronym that really opened my eyes. The acronym is HOPE—hearing other people's experiences. When I reflect on this, it feels as if the difficulties I have faced in my life can have meaning and purpose. The most impactful thing I have ever done as a communicator is share my experiences. And though not everybody would understand or agree with what I say, one thing that can't be challenged are the experiences I have walked through. When we hear other people's experiences, it gives us permission to believe that whatever we are facing, good or bad, if someone else has been able to walk through something similar to the other side, it is possible that we can do the same.

In this chapter, I share two of the most difficult experiences I have had to face in my life and how hope carried me through them.

HOPE THAT ENDURES

Ever since I was a child, I always desired to be married. This was a big deal for me, perhaps because what I saw in my mom and dad's relationship pushed me to form a more hopeful ideal for my life. Even though it wasn't my parents' example that led me to believe it was possible, I saw it through my friends' parents and their actions. I saw how they loved and cared for each other, how they sacrificed and guided their kids, and how their family was so connected. That love was attractive, and I believed that one day it might be possible for me to have that too.

We all dream of what *one day* could look like, but it rarely turns out the way that we thought it would. If I knew then what was in store for me and all I would have to go through, I'm not sure I could confidently tell you that I would have been okay with that. But when you hear someone else's story who has overcome monumental challenges in their life and you ask them how they got through it, the most common answer you hear is that they just kept going, one step at a time, never losing hope.

That is a key—never let hope get lost. If you find yourself in a place that is seemingly hopeless, the best insight I can share is this: if you feel you are going through hell, *don't stop moving forward.* If we want to think about it in terms of the road map described earlier, that place is not your exit—keep passing through. Remind your kids of this when they themselves are going through difficult times or stages in their own lives.

The day that would forever change my life for the better—the day that my hope began to turn into reality—came unexpectedly. I had started my career as a musician, and I had the privilege of sharing the stage with many incredibly talented people, and I was focused on that more than I was finding my forever partner. In 2003, I was on tour as a guitarist with an artist who would eventually become like family to me. This tour took us to the beautiful city of Calgary, Alberta, and the concert was sold out! I'll never forget that night. Four rows from the stage was a woman I made eye contact with—someone who immediately captured my heart. Her smile, her eyes, her presence, her beauty—everything about her left me speechless (and a bit distracted).

I had never experienced anything like this before. I knew that, after the concert, I needed to talk to her. When the show wrapped up, I saw her standing with a group of her friends. Not knowing what I was going to say, the only thing I could do was take one step closer to her. I am forever grateful that I didn't let fear stop me. This beautiful, intelligent, courageous, brave, and gentle soul would eventually become my wife.

When Melissa and I started our relationship, the hopes and dreams we shared were bigger than I could ever have imagined. But before we were able to chase after this life together, life had a change for us. We weren't even married yet when Melissa was diagnosed with cancer. I couldn't understand how someone so beautiful, healthy, kind, and generous would have to be marked with a sickness that had the potential to take her life. I would have done anything to transfer that pain to me. However, I had to accept that though it was not mine to take away, I could walk with her through whatever obstacles she had to face.

I could love her, support her, listen to her, cry with her, and laugh with her, but the hard truth was I could never take what was hers to endure. When we got married, she was still undergoing treatments, and during this time we were told that we would not be able to start a family. Though this was difficult to hear, I had made a commitment to love Melissa in sickness and in health, for better and for worse, no matter what.

After two rounds of surgeries, we were scheduled to see the doctor to get an update. As we sat waiting in his office, I was a bit nervous. When the doctor entered the room, he looked at me and said, "You're different than most people I meet here." I didn't know what to say, so I thanked him. He asked me why I always seemed to be happy. The only thing I could think to say was that if Melissa's illness had taught me anything, it was how precious and valuable the gift of time was, so why would I spend more of my days being upset, angry, and bitter when every moment was another gift to share with the one I loved?

He looked at me and jokingly pointed and asked, "Your wife?"

I looked over at Melissa and responded, "That one?"

"Do you have more?"

"Nope!"

And with a smile on his face, he told us that Melissa was now cancer-free. They were able to catch it in time, and the surgeries were a success. When I heard those words, I was relieved, but it also reminded me of the many people who do not get to hear that same message. I decided I would do my best to never take the gift of time for granted. As we prepared to leave the doctor's office, he wished us the very best and mentioned that if we were interested in starting a family, we had the green light. We left that office overwhelmed with the hopes and dreams we had established at the beginning of our relationship.

Shortly after the news about Melissa's health, I stopped touring and playing music and took a job at a local church helping with their youth programs. This gave me the flexibility to be available to Melissa as much as she needed me to be. And a few short months after hearing the news that we could start a family, Melissa told me that I was going to be a dad.

My first reaction was fear. If this kid was going to be anything like me when I was young—Houston, we have a problem!

I think she could tell I was nervous, so she assured me that together we could do this. Over the next little while, I settled in to feel the weight of this gift and responsibility. I knew that my life would be different, and it was now about so much more than just Melissa and me. It was now about the two of us working together to give our child the kind of life that could make the world a little brighter.

Twenty weeks into her pregnancy, things changed. We were visiting Melissa's sister when Melissa said we needed to go to the hospital. I grabbed the car keys, and off we went. I knew something wasn't right. When we arrived, nurses immediately took Melissa up to the pregnancy floor and placed a heart monitor on her. We could hear the heartbeat of our child at 155 beats per minute, and a sense of relief washed over us both. Then the doctor delivered the crushing news that it would only be a matter of time before we would stop hearing that heartbeat.

We were shattered. How do you respond to something like that? I looked at the doctor and asked if Melissa and I could have a moment alone together. When he returned, I wanted to know what we needed to do for this to work. He said we needed to reach a minimum of twenty-three weeks for there to even be a possibility for a good outcome. I don't know what came over me, but I responded, "If you want twenty-three weeks, you're getting twenty-three weeks!" We stayed in that hospital and made it to twenty-one weeks, then twenty-two weeks, and all the way to twenty-three weeks and one day. On that day, Melissa asked if I could go downstairs to get her something she was craving. While I was in the cafeteria trying to find what she wanted, Melissa called me. "Michael, get up here now," she said. "I'm about to have our baby." I took off running. When I arrived, I burst open the door. Because of the high risk of this pregnancy, there were about thirty doctors and nurses in the room with us.

The doctor led me outside the room. With his hand on my shoulder, he said, "Michael, I'm proud of you."

I didn't know how to respond, so I looked back at him and said, "I'm proud of you too, doctor!"

He smiled and continued, "If your baby's heart rate is over 100 beats per minute when it's born, we can intervene to give your child the best chance possible. But if your baby's heart rate is under 100 beats per minute, I want to encourage you to spend whatever time you have." He reassured me that whatever we chose, he'd be right there to support us. That little act of compassion meant more than that doctor will ever know.

I knew I was going to have to make a difficult decision, but it was a comfort to know that someone was there with us as we walked through one of life's most difficult moments. I stood beside Melissa, and as I held her hand, I was amazed at how incredible and miraculous the gift of life is. We didn't know if we were going to have a boy or a girl, so this was about to be a big surprise for us. On October 10, 2007, our son Jacob was born. They immediately began tests to see how he was doing. After about a minute, everyone moved out of the way so I could meet my son. When I saw him for the first time, I couldn't stop smiling. I was in awe as I stared at my baby boy. It was one of the most beautiful and powerful experiences of my life.

Then the doctor began to share some news with me. He was beating around the bush, so I stopped him, and said, "Just tell me, is he with us?"

"Yes, Michael."

"Good. Now tell me what I need to know."

He told me our baby's heart rate was only at fifty beats per minute and was dropping fast. I closed my eyes for a moment to take a breath and then looked up, and I saw that his heart rate was down to thirty-four beats per minute. I believe in miracles; however, I knew that my son was not strong enough to withstand the treatments. I asked the doctor if I could hold my son. He said, "That's the best decision you could make right now."

As I held my son, there was only one thing I wanted him to know, and that was how much his mom and dad loved him. I danced around that hospital room saying, "Jacob, your daddy loves you. Jacob, your daddy loves you." I then brought him over to Melissa and placed him in her arms. She embraced him like only a mother could do. I could feel her love for him covering every part of his being.

Every person in that room just watched as we loved our son. Nobody moved; it was as if a sacred silence had filled the room. I asked Melissa if we could do something crazy, and her response was such a gift. She said, "I trust you." So I took our son, and I asked every doctor and nurse in the room if they would like to have a chance to meet and hold him. I said, "I don't know how much time we have, but you've been chosen to share this moment with us, and we would like to share this moment with you." I passed our son to the first doctor, and Melissa and I watched as he made a difference in the lives of all the people in the room.

For twenty-four minutes, heaven kissed earth. Twenty-four minutes later, when Jacob made his way back to me, he took his last breath, and our son was heaven-bound. He never spoke a word or made a difference through a deliberate action. His still, small presence was enough. Enough to help and inspire countless others through the miracle of his story.

As I write this, I am still overwhelmed with emotions and questions, many of which I accept may never have answers. However, since that day, I recognized that the amount of time was not the difficult part. Of course, I would have given anything to have had more time with him. The hardest part was realizing how often I take for granted the time I do have for the people I love.

When I share this story with teenagers, I conclude it with this challenge. Jacob was with us for only twenty-four minutes, and today, you and I have been given twenty-four hours. Whatever we choose to do with this gift is completely up to us. This is our invitation to do whatever we must, to make right with the people we love. The time starts now!

FINAL THOUGHTS

Your kids desperately want to know and hear how much they mean to you. You are the greatest influence in your child's life, and there is nothing more important than recognizing this reality. When we choose to put our egos aside and disconnect their actions from our parenting, we find peace and hope that gives us the confidence to know that they are learning just as we did. They are still in process. And they need us now more than ever to be a light in their darkest moments, an embrace when they need to feel safe, and their hope when things feel uncertain.

What can you do today that will help your kid feel they are a valued priority in your life? This is your opportunity to share your experiences that have brought you to where you are today. This is wisdom that has been given to you as a gift to share with your children so they can become better equipped to handle similar situations. As you continue your mission, lean on the gift of time and the gift of your family that has been entrusted to you.

ACCEPT

We don't have forever to spend with our kids living at home with us—every moment is precious. We must accept that our kids will grow up and grow beyond the limits we place on them. What they do and choose in life will be in part how we as parents provided an anchor of hope when they needed it most, especially when the situation was hard and uncomfortable to bring to the light.

REFLECT

The fleeting moments we share with our children under our care pass faster than we often comprehend. Within these hours, days, and years, a profound story is being written and begins with the statement, "Because of you . . . ." The words that follow are ours to shape, and breathe life into.

This narrative will be told from the perspective of our kids, and it's our mission, our responsibility, to ensure that the continuation of that statement resounds with themes of hope, connection, understanding, authenticity, and unconditional love. The gift of this sacred responsibility was bestowed on you, and you chose to honor this gift by giving your all, by giving your very best. Your commitment and resilience are undeniable, and you have maintained an undefeated record in facing life's difficulties. As your children prepare to step into the next phase of their lives, remember this fundamental truth: You are, and always will be, the greatest influence in your kid's life.

CONNECT

Do whatever you can to make sure your child knows and believes that whatever happens in their life, you will always be there to love, listen, guide, and support them (even if it's hard; even if it hurts). Here are some things to consider:

- They are never too young or old to need a hug.
- Be encouraging even when things are tough.
- Tell your kids you love them each and every day.

- Your time with them and the hope you create are crucial priorities. Things will happen that may require you to put your reputation, work, and friendships at stake. This relationship you have been entrusted with is more important than anything else you may be known for. Your children know you better than most ever will, and your presence and care for them will become an anchor of hope within them. As your kids step into the world as adults, they will reflect back and see the heroic and selfless sacrifices you made for them.

THINGS I WISH MY PARENTS KNEW . . .

I'm sorry I keep messing up. I feel that I am always trying to be perfect, and all you see is what I do wrong. It would be helpful to know that you see some things that I am doing right.

—

Sometimes I just need a hug.

TEN

Giving and Forgiving

I'll confess—I am very easily distracted. The number of times my dad told me to pay attention and stay focused could have been his most repeated parenting advice. Typically, I'd nod in agreement and move on, but on the day I got my driver's license, I saw a new level of uncertainty in his eyes. He was trying, I could see, to look happy on the outside and not to show his fear—fear not only for himself but for everyone else on the road.

That was also the year I received a music scholarship to attend a prestigious private school in Houston, Texas. It was not unknown to the other students that I was there on a scholarship and did not have many of the same privileges as my classmates. My first day was a bit unsettling. Though I didn't know a soul there, I had always been up for a challenge, and I had a decision to make: own the opportunity or let others decide and dictate how I would be treated and perceived. I chose the first option, and I had to intentionally make that decision every single day of that school year.

I noticed that just about everyone in my grade was starting to drive themselves to school. Many times, classmates asked me when I was going to get a car. Even though I was now an official licensed driver, having my own car was not in the cards. I saw how much my dad worked, and he did his best to provide a good life for the both of us, but I knew he couldn't afford to buy me a car. I also felt that asking for something like this would add more pressure on him, and that did not seem fair.

My real motive for wanting a car was more for an opportunity than a luxury. Two years before receiving my license, I began playing music professionally. I knew a car would not only enable me to go out and share my gift but also give me opportunities to develop it. I had no idea how this dream would become a reality, so the only thing I could think to do was to pray for it. After offering up my request, I felt at peace with whatever the outcome would be.

As much as I did not want to tell my dad about my little dream, he knew—parents always seem to know. He brought it up, and I was relieved that he did. "I want so bad to be able to get you a car, but things are a bit tight, so here's what I can offer: If you can promise to pay attention and stay focused, you can use my car." The car he was talking about was an old white station wagon with baby-blue leather seats—so classic. I thanked him and promised to do my best to "pay attention and stay focused." I also told him that I had prayed for a car. His response was "Well, you always seem to find a way to make things work, and I couldn't think of anyone better to have one." That response encouraged me more than he would ever know.

Over the next few weeks at my new school, it was clear that I would likely only last for one school year—the academic side was far beyond my current ability to keep up. The teachers and staff were beyond gracious and offered as much help as they could. One of the counselors sat with me and asked if I had considered what I would do after high school.

I knew I wanted to help people, and the best way I knew how was through music and telling stories. She spoke into me a new confidence that day. "I have rarely met someone with your ability to connect with people and make them feel the way you do. I understand your grades do not reflect your God-given ability, and I want you to set yourself up to accomplish what I see is bigger than you can probably imagine." As gracefully as she could, she let me know that the scholarship would only be for the remainder of this year. As the news sank in, I was expecting to feel defeated, embarrassed, and rejected, but instead I felt relieved, seen, and excited for whatever the next year would look like.

A few days later, I was approached by one of the secretaries at the school. She was always very kind to me and obviously knew that my time at the school was coming to an end. She unexpectedly asked, "Michael, if you could have anything, what would you want?" Not knowing how to answer, I stumbled out a superficial reply. Sensing my confusion, she explained that her family wanted to do something special for me and again asked, "What is something you would like to have that may seem impossible to get?"

I felt stunned and a bit nervous about how to even respond. After an awkward moment of silence, she said she believed I was going to do some great things. "But to do them," she said, "how do you plan to get yourself there? Do you have a car?"

"No," I answered, "but that's one of my dreams, so hopefully one day soon."

"I like your dream. Can you please follow me outside?"

My heart began to pound as I followed her. Outside was parked a 1988 Chevy Suburban with the front door open. Shock, gratitude, and disbelief washed over me.

"Do you like it?" she asked.

"*Like* it? This is unbelievable."

"Michael, this has been a gift to our family for the past ten years, and today our gift now becomes your gift, with no strings attached. We will miss you here at our school, but I believe that what God has in store for you will lead you to help many people. This gift is our way to help you on that journey."

GENEROSITY, TWOFOLD

That school taught me what generosity looks and feels like. I am thankful to have had the privilege to spend the time I had at Houston Christian High School—Go Mustangs!

My dad couldn't believe I had a Suburban—and neither could I. Again, he made it clear that I must be careful. "Please pay attention and stay focused," he said.

Fast-forward to my final year of high school. I was driving into the parking lot, waving at all my friends. I saw a parking spot that was front and center, and as usual, I was trying to make people smile and laugh as I made faces pulling into this spot, and then *bam!*

I completely crushed the car that was parked in the stall next to mine. *Oh my goodness, this did not just happen.* I was now the spotlit center of attention, and everyone's jaw almost hit the floor. There was no way out of this one. Not only was this beyond embarrassing, but when I saw the car I hit, I was sick to my stomach. The person who owned it was known to have a temper and the ability to use her words to make just about anybody feel like a bag of garbage. I always felt bad for her because of what people said about her. Although I didn't know her well, she was always kind to me—thankfully!

Now it was time for me to get out of the car and make the walk of embarrassment through the front doors of the school. In my typical way, I decided to make a better moment of it, so when my foot hit the ground, I held both hands high in the air and started clapping. The roar of what seemed like a stadium joined in, and as I walked through the door of the school, I knew what had to be done. I immediately found the girl whose car I hit and asked, "Sooo, how is your day going?"

"Good. Michael, what do you want?"

"Well, your day might get a little worse because I just hit your car." I was now ready to receive all that I deserved, but after a few deep breaths, she looked at me, smiled, and said, "I really didn't like that car much anyway. But will you or your parents be able to fix it?" I promised to make sure it would be taken care of. She smiled, and that was that. *Whew!* I was speechless at what had just happened.

It was the next call that I had to make that I was really dreading, but it had to be done. When I picked up the pay phone (for those younger people reading this, google it), every ring seemed like an eternity. Finally, on the other end of the line I heard my dad's voice.

"Dad, um, something just happened, and I'm scared to tell you, but I just wrecked the car in the parking lot at school." My hands were shaking, and my heart was about to beat out of my chest. His next question was the most important but loving question he could have asked: "Son, are you okay?"

I wasn't expecting that, and when I heard those words, I broke down. "Yes, Dad, I'm okay."

"Well, all is good! We all make mistakes, and I'm thankful nobody is hurt. I'll head to the school and figure out what needs to be done. Everything will be okay, and I promise we will figure it out."

As I hung up the phone, I was relieved, but also aware that if I had been paying attention and focused on what I was doing, this accident would have never happened.

What was memorable for me was that when I got home, and my dad and I sat down for dinner, he said nothing about me wrecking the car. Was he losing his memory?

"So . . . about today," I started.

"What about it?"

"Really?"

"Michael, we all make mistakes. I'm sure you thought about what you could have done differently, and I'm confident that you will not forget the lesson you just learned. When you called me, I didn't care about anything other than knowing you were okay. Once that was clear to me, I knew the other problems were small, and I've already taken care of them. But, Michael, before we move on from this, what did you learn?"

I was so ready to answer this: "Pay attention and stay focused."

"Perfect—you nailed it! Because the cost of not doing so will always cost more than you think."

PATIENCE, PRESENCE, AND FORGIVENESS

When you were a kid, did you ever think, *When I grow up, and I have kids . . .* ? Chances are, it crossed some of our minds at some point when we were young. If you're among those of us who've entertained this thought, how did you honestly think that would play out? Perhaps you had some notion of being a giving and forgiving parent who was always patient, understanding, and fun. This is far from most experiences and honestly a bit naïve. That's because, as kids, we can never know how hard this is for our parents to pull off. But my father shared with me the gifts of patience and forgiveness that day. Whenever I become impatient with my own children, I remind myself of his gifts to me and his capacity for grace and forgiveness.

As parents, the ability to adapt is huge. What once was a clear way to help our kids understand or learn something does not always have the same impact as they get older, and we have to adjust our parenting. We feel ourselves wanting to impart more responsibility and expect more from them as they get older. But by this time, they have also most likely learned exactly what they need to say or do to get you off their back. This is usually followed by the quiet mumbling of something like "You just don't understand," or worse and often regretted, "I hate you."

As a parent, being "giving and forgiving" in these trying times is huge!

What if that isn't enough? How do we know if we are making progress when things seem disconnected and the relationship with our child feels distant?

We continue to show up and make ourselves present and available. Our presence becomes a reminder to them that even when life is confusing, frustrating, and unfair, we choose to be present and visible for them.

THE TIME WE ARE GIVEN

In August 2017, I found myself flying down to Texas once again, but this time, things were different. My dad was facing a serious health crisis. He had developed a tumor on his leg that had grown to the size of a softball, and surgery was inevitable. I flew down to be with him, knowing the situation was serious and my being there would be a support for him.

When I arrived, I drove him straight to the hospital, and the doctors immediately scheduled his surgery. It was a tense time, but my dad told me he was grateful I was there with him. Then we received another piece of devastating news. My grandmother—my dad's mother—had passed away. Growing up, she had been the most loving and encouraging person in my life.

The timing couldn't have been worse. Adding even more intensity to all of this, Hurricane Harvey was heading straight for Texas, and the entire region was on high alert. Airports were closing, and my wife and kids were unable to fly down for the funeral. It was a difficult time, made even harder by the fact that my family couldn't be there with me.

The funeral had to be rushed because of the hurricane, and everything felt like it was happening too fast. I had been asked to speak at the service, but I wasn't sure I could do it. The weight of everything was overwhelming. But as I stood at the podium and looked out into the crowd of family and close friends—what stood out most was my dad's face. He gave me a look I'll never forget—a look that said, "I'm proud of you." And that was all I needed to get through it.

After the funeral, we returned to my cousin's house to wait out the hurricane. With the floodwaters rising, we were completely trapped. We found solace in one another's company. My dad, cousins, and Aunt Bonnie spent days together, cut off from the outside world. We shared stories and memories, we laughed, and we reconnected in ways that might not have happened under different circumstances.

It's funny how we find ourselves in places that at first look to be too much to handle and then find something worthwhile through the experience. This reminds us that the moments that seem the most challenging often turn out to be the most meaningful. Those days spent with my family, waiting out the storm, turned into a gift of time that I will cherish and forever hold close.

On the morning of August 30, 2017, everything changed.

It was around 4:00 a.m. when I heard my dad calling my name. I am usually a deep sleeper, but I woke up immediately with my heart pounding. I rushed to where he was sleeping and found him having a medical emergency. The situation was dire, and I knew we needed help fast. The paramedics arrived quickly—well, fairly quickly, because of the fact that I sent them to the wrong address at first. (I apologize to the family I do not know, but if you live in Sour Lake, Texas, and are still wondering what that was all about, my bad.) The flooding from the hurricane was so crazy that driving to the hospital was not an option.

That's when one of the paramedics made a call for an emergency airlift. Within an hour, a medical helicopter arrived, landing on one of the few roads that hadn't been completely submerged by the floods. It felt like a miracle.

I was allowed to accompany my dad on the helicopter, and as we took off, we had no idea where we were headed. The captain decided on Galveston, Texas, as it was the closest and best option. My first thought was *Wait, Galveston is on the Gulf of Mexico, and the hurricane is full on—is this the best plan?* He assured me that this was the best option and would be best for Dad. The whole ride I held my dad's hand. I knew these might be our final moments together, and I wanted to make sure I said everything I needed to say. I told him how much I loved him, how grateful I was for everything he had done for me, and how proud I was to be his son, and I was able to say a prayer with him.

My dad smiled weakly and squeezed my hand. "Michael," he whispered, "I love you so much. I'm so proud of you. I'm thankful to be your dad."

Those were the last words my dad ever said to me. Later that evening, at 9:30 p.m., he passed away.

In the days that followed, I found myself reflecting on the lessons my dad had taught me over the years. Losing someone close to you changes your perspective on life. It makes you realize how precious life is and how fleeting it can be. Every moment we have with the people we love is a gift, and we can't afford to take it for granted.

After my dad's passing, we sold the house I had grown up in. It was a difficult decision, and I hadn't anticipated the flood of emotions that would come with it. That house held so many memories and always felt like a safe home base I could go back to.

A few months after the house was sold, I flew down to Houston for a speaking engagement. On my way to the event, I decided to stop by my old neighborhood. I pulled up in front of the house and got out of the car, and standing at the edge of the street, I remembered the time my dad told me as a kid not to go in the street.

But this time, things were different. The house no longer belonged to me. The grass, the street, the memories—they were all still there, but the house itself was no longer mine. If I had stepped on that grass, I would have been literally trespassing.

That's when I realized something profound. Just as I could no longer step on that property as it was no longer presently mine, my access to what was familiar and comfortable had to change. This also goes for forgiveness; once we forgive, we release all that can prevent us from moving forward. Every time we go back to that old way of thinking, we are literally trespassing into feelings and emotions that no longer have power or ownership attached to us. This idea is a powerful reminder to be careful not to use anything from our child's past as a weapon to shame or scold them with in the present.

FINAL THOUGHTS

As parents, it's easy to hold on to the mistakes our kids make. We remind them of their failures, sometimes without even realizing it, and we hold those moments over their heads like a cloud, resulting in resentment and shame. But what I've learned, both as a son and as a father, is that we can't keep trespassing into a past that no longer exists.

Our kids' mess-ups and missteps should never become a spotlight for all to see and judge. Others will not have full context, and a major part of our responsibility as a parent is to protect. Our kids are not their mistakes. If we continue to focus on these shortfalls as a way to "protect" an image of ourselves we want others to see, we have created a separation that could take a lifetime to restore. Be assured that your reputation, the need to be right, or the pressure to always be perfect holds zero weight compared to the realization of how important and significant this relationship truly is.

Instead, we must choose to see the good, to celebrate the growth, and to focus on the present. Today is "day one." It's the day we start fresh, giving ourselves permission to reframe how we see our past—not as a bad thing, but rather as our proven record of victory. This will bring a passion and joy into our present to help us to rediscover the miracle of this exact moment.

For me, that's the lesson I've carried with me since my dad's passing. It's the lesson I work to instill in my own children, and it's the lesson I hope others will embrace and see the value of.

We all make mistakes, but we are not our mistakes. We are so much more than that. This brings us to a decision point. We can choose to let our past define us and hold us back, or we can choose to create a greater future because of what our past has taught us.

I choose a greater future, and I hope you will too.

ACCEPT

We all make mistakes; our kids are not one of them. Help them discover the good, true, and beautiful we know and see in them.

REFLECT

Ask yourself, "What have I learned from my parents that I am grateful for today?"

CONNECT

Consider keeping a journal of what inspires you about your kid. Whether it's daily, weekly, or monthly, start today. This will become an incredible gift that your child will cherish and be thankful for. If your child is already grown up, you can still take some time to write about all the great things you see and have learned from them.

Decide on a good time to give this gift, such as a graduation, birthday, or special day they are celebrating, and I am confident it will be a gift that will bring you all closer together. Remember to:

- Thank your child when they share with you something you see was difficult for them to do.
- Show your child what you do for work and explain why you choose to give your time to do this job.
- Surprise your child by showing up somewhere they least expect to see you (even just to say hello).
- Create a distraction-free amount of time every day to be present and available for each other—your child has a lot you can learn from.
- Let them see you have fun and invite them to join in.
- Encourage them to try new things that will push them to discover what they are capable of.
- When they make a mistake, ask them why they felt they had to make that decision.

CONCLUSION

I have chosen to complete this book by sharing what these letters have inspired in me. As a father, there is nothing more important than my kids knowing that my love for them is greater than any mistake they could ever make. I have learned how much our kids are yearning to have a relationship with us that is real, authentic, and free. The expectations they feel can seem impossible to reach, which often leads them to retreat into silence, believing there is nothing they could say or do that could be enough. This unspoken decision not only fractures how they see themselves but also creates a separation in the relationship with their parents.

Through the challenges they face—school, friendships, relationships, technology, extracurricular activities, and their ever-busy schedules—it's no wonder that finding peace can feel impossible. The pressure to perform well in all these areas would overwhelm anyone without guided direction. This is where we begin to see the difference between performance and potential. When we focus solely on evaluating or rewarding performance—whether through grades, trophies, following rules, or doing what we ask without questioning or arguing—we risk overlooking their untapped potential waiting to emerge.

Your child's potential is a masterpiece waiting to be discovered.

Encourage their curiosity, wonder, and independence—you'll be amazed at what you begin to see.

I plead with every parent reading this to take the time to define what your family mission and values are. Ensure that everyone understands the core values, knows they are nonnegotiable, and recognizes how each person can contribute to the mission. This is so important because when mistakes are made and lines are crossed, it eliminates confusion about what will happen next. It shows us that the next step is always restoration—not just making things as they were but making them better.

Our personalities, gifts, and talents are all unique, confirming that we each have something special to offer. At the same time, we all have something to learn from one another—such as how different it is to be a high school student today compared to when we were in school. The world of technology and social media has connected this generation faster than anything in existence before, yet it has also opened a door to overwhelming comparison and a flood of information that has left many kids feeling as though they can never measure up—or worse, unsee what they've encountered.

We cannot assume that our kids understand what we mean or expect from them. Just as in business, a mission statement and list of core values must be constantly reinforced to avoid becoming empty slogans—we must frequently revisit and reinforce the principles in our families. The time and energy we dedicate to our jobs and external goals often outweigh the time and attention we give to our relationships, especially with our kids. It's time we evaluate where we stand, personally, relationally, and professionally, as it relates to our family. From there, it becomes our responsibility to change whatever we must to restore the truth, goodness, and beauty our family needs and deserves.

You've got this!

Writing this book has felt like holding up a mirror, showing me clearly the many things I'd love to change and make better if I could. Every story shared here matters deeply to me, each drawn from my personal experiences from different chapters of my life. I've come to realize that there's always more to each story than my limited viewpoint. Still, these experiences profoundly shaped how I saw myself and my place in the world. Honestly, it has taken me many years to unlearn old patterns and understand that the past doesn't have to control how I create a better present and future for my family.

As parents, we should remind ourselves what it was like when we were growing up—wanting freedom, craving trust, and wishing our parents could understand us without always needing to correct or instruct. It's also important, and a bit humbling, to remember how much we kept hidden from our own parents, often afraid of their reactions. Thinking about these experiences has deeply inspired me to write this book. My hope is that none of us look back wishing we had listened more patiently, shown more empathy, or simply been more present and available to our children. This will lead us to approach our children with compassion rather than criticism, supporting them through challenges and celebrating their progress, rather than focusing only on their mistakes or what we assume they think we expect of them.

I think deep down, we all want a meaningful, lasting connection with our children. But sometimes, despite our best intentions, we fall short and feel disappointed in ourselves. For example, we often spend long hours working hard to provide for our families, which can mean missing out on special moments—moments that could have become treasured memories shared across generations.

I know it's not always easy to be the kind of parent we'd like to be—always available, always patient, always understanding. Life gets complicated, and sometimes we're stretched thin. Still, I encourage you not to let these challenges become reasons or excuses to disengage. Ultimately, we will always make time for the things we truly care about. Our children look up to us, absorbing our values and beliefs, shaping their own identities from what they see and feel in us.

Music has been a powerful way for my family to connect and share what we often struggle to say in words. As I've mentioned earlier, my father was an accomplished musician, and he passed that love of music to me. Now, as I watch my own children grow, I see them discovering their gifts in ways that amaze me, surpassing even what I could do at their age. My teenage daughter, Hannah, has written songs that genuinely move me—songs that speak directly to the heart. Naturally, as her dad, I might be biased, but my years in the music industry have taught me to recognize when someone has a genuine talent—a special ability that can truly touch others. Hannah, without question, has that incredible gift.

I made a conscious decision not to push my own path or passions on my kids. Even though I saw Hannah's musical talent early on, what I'm most thankful for is that I took the time to really listen—to her lyrics, her melodies, her heart. In her songs, I began to hear things she couldn't say out loud: her hopes, her struggles, and the emotions she was unsure how to share face-to-face. She may have been afraid of how I'd react, worried about letting me down, or simply unsure if I was present enough to truly hear her. But through her music, she found her voice—and I found a deeper way to know and understand my daughter.

I encourage you, as one parent to another, to really notice and honor the one-of-a-kind light in your kids—their talents, quirks, and the things that light them up. Pay close attention to the small ways they try to express themselves, even when it's not obvious or easy to understand. Often, these moments are their way of letting us into their world. Meet them there, with humility and an open heart. Love and guide them where they are, not where you think they should be, and let them know you're with them every step of the way.

What I've come to believe with everything in me is this: our children are always trying to tell us something—sometimes with words, sometimes through music or art, and other times through silence, frustration, or even chaos. However it shows up, it's their way of letting us into what's going on inside. These moments aren't just random behaviors—they're invitations. When we slow down, pay attention, and lean in with genuine curiosity, we begin to truly see where they are and what they're trying to share with us—what they need, what they feel, and what they hope we'll understand. And when our kids feel seen, heard, and accepted—especially in the moments when they don't quite have the words—it deepens the foundation of trust and love that helps them never question or fear coming to us when they need it most. It becomes part of the story they carry into adulthood: the story of a parent who took the time to understand, who chose connection over constant correction, and who loved them even when they felt misunderstood, overwhelmed, or unsure of themselves—a parent who didn't need them to be perfect, just present, and who stayed close and connected no matter what.

—

The final story I want to share brings me so much joy. My son, Simon, has been one of my biggest encouragers throughout the journey of writing this book. Every day for the past few months, he's asked, "Are you done yet? Are you done yet?"

Over time, I started to feel like the finish line was moving further away. He could sense the weight of it on me and even offered to sit with me and type my words if I would simply tell him what to write. His support has meant the world to me as I wrestled through this process. But today, I fully understood just how deep his love runs.

Simon needs his dad to be fully present. And the truth is, you can't fake real presence—not when work, no matter how meaningful, keeps you so busy and distracted that you miss moments you'll never get back. Without realizing it, he was setting aside his own needs so I wouldn't feel any added pressure. That wasn't okay.

I began to notice something: every time I finished a chapter or a story, he would visibly see the relief and gratitude on my face. And in those moments, he finally felt free enough to show me whatever he was excited about. All he ever wanted was my attention and presence. After just a few minutes of undivided focus, his cup was full. And then, almost immediately, he'd encourage me to keep going and finish the book.

That's when it hit me: We often convince ourselves that finishing a project, making more money, or accumulating more stuff will somehow create more time. But there will always be another project. There will always be a reason more money would be helpful. And we likely already have more than we need.

What we will never have again is today's date.

May we never forget how rich we are to be given another 86,400 seconds.

When I grow up, I hope to have a heart like Simon's—one that loves so selflessly, that gives without condition, and that knows the greatest gift we can offer is our presence.

—

I want to thank you for journeying with me—through my life and through the letters that have been shared. My hope is that you receive this as a gift, something to be discovered and reflected on.

I understand that some stories may resonate more deeply than others and that what you've learned might challenge what you already know. Please know that my heart and intention are simply this: for you to see and believe that your role as a parent is, and always will be, one of the greatest influences in your child's life.

With that, I wish you the very best as you continue to build a life and family that your children will cherish forever. May the stories our kids tell about us in the future begin with "Because of you . . ."—showing future generations what it truly means to be seen, understood, supported, and above all, loved.

APPENDIX

ADDITIONAL LETTERS TO PARENTS

I LOVE YOU

"That I really love them. I care for them, that I am blessed to have parents like them."

–

"How much I appreciate them. How much I love them."

–

"That I love them so much."

–

"I love my family so much, I wish they could know all my dark secrets, but I would rather them know how much I thank them for never giving up on me."

–

"I wish my parents knew they are the most amazing individuals. All heart, all passion, all love. I love them so much, and I cherish them forever."

I LOVE YOU

"They are doing a wonderful job raising and teaching both my brother and me. They are truly amazing and give me everything I need. I owe all my success to them. Without them, I wouldn't be where I am today. They truly are the best."

—

"I hope they know that even if I don't always say it, I love them."

—

"I love them as much as I love God."

—

"I want to spend more time with them because I love them so much; I just don't know what to say sometimes."

—

"I love them even when they think I hate them."

—

"I wish they knew how much I love them, even when I'm yelling. It's not hate, it's hurt."

WHAT I STRUGGLE TO SAY

"Most times, I'm afraid that I won't even talk to you when I'm older because we argue so much."

—

"I wish my parents knew how I feel on the inside."

—

"I wish I could tell my parents what is really happening in my life . . . but I'm scared."

—

"The only reason I talk back is because I get scared. I get so anxious all the time, and I don't know how to talk about it or make it better."

—

"Sometimes I think you don't love me because of your tone of voice."

—

"When they fight, it doesn't just affect them. It affects me, too. I get scared they'll leave."

WHAT I STRUGGLE TO SAY

"I want them to know it's hard to be open with them when I know they'd take it the wrong way and get mad."

—

"I feel excluded sometimes. I feel left out. I get sad. I am depressed and lonely, but [my parents] make me feel better at the end of every day. I want them to know that I understand and see how much they do for me and how much they sacrifice for me."

—

"Dad, please listen when I try to talk to you and don't brush me off."

—

"When I struggle with depression, it's not your fault."

—

"The way you talk about me to your friends really hurts."

WHAT I FEEL

"When you say, 'I can talk to you about anything,' I expect that you will be calm and try to understand my situation."

—

"That criticizing me over everything I do does ***not*** *inspire me to do better; it only makes me do worse and still lowers my confidence and makes me feel worse about myself."*

—

"I wish they sympathized with me and didn't tell me to get over myself. I wish they knew how lonely I feel."

—

"I wish my parents knew that balancing my mental health, social life, and my academics is not easy. I'm tired of feeling the same way over and over. I wish they would try to see my perspective sometimes. We all make mistakes, so please don't treat us like it's the worst mistake—you were all teenagers once, too."

—

"I'm not perfect, but I try my best. I wish they could see that."

WHAT I FEEL

"I wish they knew that I feel they only see my mistakes."

—

"I think my parents are doing a good job, but sometimes I don't think they take my feelings into account."

—

"Even though sometimes they can't see through my behavior, I wish they would."

—

"My faith is really important to me, and I wish you would not make fun of me about it."

—

"I am so scared of disappointing you."

—

"Your divorce wasn't just hard on you; it is hard on me too."

—

"Sometimes I just want to disappear. The pressure is too much."

WHAT I NEED FROM YOU

"I wish my parents knew that I want to spend more time with them."

—

"I wish my mom knew that I want her to be my mom and best friend!"

—

"That I am more than my report card."

—

"I want my parents to know that because of their support, my depression has eased and I'm still alive."

—

"Parents should know how important it is to greet their children whenever they see them; it's so uplifting whenever I get a smile in the morning; it affects my whole day."

—

"That allowing your child to just talk, and you just listen, is the best support."

WHAT I NEED FROM YOU

"I want my parents to know how worthless I feel."

—

"I want faith like Dad and kindness like Mom."

—

"I just wish we could be as close as we once were, without feeling controlled."

—

"I wish you were more honest with me and yourself."

—

"I want us to have a family picture."

—

"I wish my parents knew how hard it is to be expected to love someone when I don't even love myself."

WHAT I NEED FROM YOU

"I appreciate everything my mom does for me and that just because I chose to live with Dad doesn't mean I love her less."

—

"I wish they knew how much I love them but find it hard to say."

—

"I hope to make them prouder every day because I am trying my best."

—

"I want them to know that I would do anything to make them happy."

—

"I have a passion for singing and dancing; I want to be a singer when I grow up; I can really use my skills in modeling, singing, acting, and dancing; I'm too scared to tell them that this is what I really want. I just want them to be happy even if I have to give up my dreams."

WHAT I NEED FROM YOU

"All the support you've given me in the past fourteen years has helped me become who I am."

—

"I only feel I can talk about what is allowed to be talked about. How will you know that I have tried to end everything and still sometimes feel that way? When you found out I was struggling, you told me how selfish that would be if I ever went through with it. I have never felt so hurt that you never asked why I even felt this way. I need you to know that I forgive you and hope I can be honest and share about how my life is really going today."

—

"I wish they'd listen instead of always trying to fix me."

—

"Let me be who I am, not who you want me to be."

WHAT I WANT FOR AND FROM YOU

"I want you to know that everything I do is to make you proud."

—

"I want you to understand that when you come into my room without knocking, many times this has made me feel very uncomfortable. I will always let you in, but please for the love of all things good—just knock."

—

"I want you to know that I see all you have done and sacrifice for me and that makes me feel very loved."

—

"I want you to listen and not always try to fix me."

—

"My mom and dad are too busy for me to tell them what I need."

WHAT I WANT FOR AND FROM YOU

"I need a break from my phone! Please help!"

—

"Why won't you tell me about what it was like when you were growing up? I want to know everything."

—

"I hear you fighting every night, and I feel it's my fault you two don't get along."

—

"I promise to get better. I love you more than anything in the world."

—

"I want them to trust me. I'm not perfect, but I'm not reckless."

—

"I wish I could admit my mistakes without getting yelled at."

—

"I've made mistakes. Please don't hold them against me forever."

IT'S YOUR TURN

Don't hold back here—you have permission to be as raw and honest as you are willing to be. What do you wish your parents knew?

—

With gratitude and joy for you, and your future, please finish this statement and, when ready, share with your child: Things I wish my child knew . . .

ABOUT THE AUTHOR

Photo by Yuan Wang

MICHAEL CHIASSON is a dynamic creator in the art of public speaking, music, television, and writing, with a career that spans more than twenty-five years. His compelling and personal approach has inspired over five hundred thousand people across North America.

As the visionary behind the Chiasson Group and founder of a Canadian registered charity, Access52 (access52.com), Michael has championed the belief that people thrive when they have a clear vision of who they are, what they're capable of, and how they can make their greatest contribution. Michael also holds a diploma in leadership and sacred studies.

Beyond his work as a communicator, he treasures what is most important to him with his wife, Melissa, and their two children, Hannah and Simon.